CLASSIC AMERICAN
SEMI TRUCKS

Jeremy Lipschultz and Stan Holtzman

MBI Publishing Company

First published in 2000 by MBI Publishing Company, 729 Prospect Avenue, PO Box 1, Osceola, WI 54020-0001 USA

The information in this book is true and complete to the best of our knowledge. All recommendations are made without any guarantee on the part of the author or Publisher, who also disclaim any liability incurred in connection with the use of this data or specific details.

We recognize that some words, model names and designations, for example, mentioned herein are the property of the trademark holder. We use them for identification purposes only. This is not an official publication.

MBI Publishing Company books are also available at discounts in bulk quantity for industrial or sales-promotional use. For details write to Special Sales Manager at Motorbooks International Wholesalers & Distributors, 729 Prospect Avenue, PO Box 1, Osceola, WI 54020-0001 USA.

Library of Congress Cataloging-in-Publication Data
Lipschultz, Jeremy Harris.
    Classic American semi-trucks / Jeremy Harris Lipschultz and Stan Holtzman.
        p. cm.
    Includes index.

ISBN 0-7603-0825-X (pbk. : alk. paper)
    1. Tractor Trailer combination—United States. I. Holtzman, Stan. II. Title
TL230.5.T73 L57   2000
629.224—dc21   00-028175

On the front cover: Brooks Carroll of Cave Creek, Arizona, hauls livestock with this extended hood KW. Around 1985, Kenworth decided to discontinue the long-hood model, but by 1990 it realized that it was losing sales to Peterbilt, as truckers still demanded the long-hood conventionals. The W900L soon came out to challenge the Peterbilt Model 379, and it was one of the best decisions the folks at Kenworth ever made.

On the frontispiece: A 1940s low-mount Peterbilt sits in an open field in Hemet, California, awaiting restoration.

On the title page: A 1949 Autocar with a Cummins 262-horsepower engine, backed by a five-speed main and three-speed auxiliary transmission, is seen in this 1970 picture, pulling for Johnny Teresi Trucking of Lodi, California.

On the back cover: Two of the most famous big-rig nameplates ever to cross the American road belong to Diamond T and Peterbilt.

Edited by Keith Mathiowetz
Designed by Bruce Leckie

Printed in China

CONTENTS

INTRODUCTION

You know, I really like to drive trucks. It's a great life. I'd work for nothing as long as I had a good truck and trailer and a good run. But don't tell my boss about willing to work for nothing.
—anonymous truck driver (1979)

The American semi-truck is responsible for literally driving the most prosperous economy the world has ever known. Americans today have access to more goods at lower prices than any previous people, and this change has created abundance and wealth for a majority of its citizens. Trucks and their drivers are the unsung heroes of this economic revolution; we take for granted seemingly unlimited access to consumer products. The rise of motor vehicles, including automobiles and trucks, coincided in the 1920s with the development of consumerism—an American invention driven by advertising and modern mass media. Once the Industrial Revolution had made it possible to manufacture goods for a mass market, the people needed to be sold. Trucking was one important element in the rise of the American marketplace. Even at the dawning of the so-called "information age," the transport of physical materials remained central. Electronic commerce may be conducted on the Internet, but purchases are delivered via the trucking industry. As the American Trucking Association once boasted, "If you bought it, a truck brought it." In America, the semi-truck has been the vital link between where a product is produced and where it is consumed. The growth and efficiency of trucking has powered our booming economy, particularly in the deregulatory environment of the 1990s.

This book is about the American semi-truck. Its focus is on the makes and models that helped define trucks and trucking during what might be called "the first century." Trucking is part of a larger development of transportation in this country that included the boat, the train, the automobile, the airplane, and even interstate pipelines. But it is the development of trucks in the second half of the century, along with the growth of the interstate highway system, that forever changed the way we think about ourselves and our world.

By some estimates, the transportation of goods accounts for about 20 percent of the American economy. "Trucking is by far the most important sector of the industry," writes economist Paul Teske and his associates, "generating more than three-quarters of the revenues of the freight transport industry." Railroads are a distant second, passed long ago by the big rigs of the highway. The truck seemed to fit the American notion of freedom, as well as the urge to keep moving. As writer James Thomas has observed, trucking has its roots in the culture of the wagon train, stagecoach, steamboat, and railroad. Transportation, then, went hand in hand with communication among places: "The arrival of these cargo carriers in isolated communities often was the most exciting event of the day, week, or even month. News of the outside world could be had, scarce merchandise could be purchased, and tales of exotic places could be heard." The social revolution of the horseless carriage, and the decline of agricultural life, meant that people rapidly became less isolated—particularly with the advent of communication technologies such as the telephone, radio, and television. But it was trucking, and the drive to create a nationwide network of highways, that really connected the nation.

No longer did goods and commodities have to move by railroad. Trucks were not confined to narrow ribbons of steel, and truckers could serve both city and countryside with transportation services. Truckers did not halt their vehicles at the end of the paved road but extended their routes over dirt tracks. And once again, the public imagination had found a romantic hero.

A drug store in downtown Sperry, Oklahoma, typifies what America is all about. All of America relies on trucks for its very existence, and this is especially true of the small towns that dot this nation.

James Thomas contends that truckers captured the imagination of a generation of young boys who grew up to follow a dream of being a mythical cowboy on the road:

> AT EACH SLEEPY HAMLET, SMALL BOYS WERE AWESTRUCK AT THE SIGHT OF LARGE, SPUTTERING, SMOKING TRUCKS. WHILE THEIR FATHERS ASKED QUESTIONS ABOUT THE MECHANICAL ASPECTS . . . THE BOYS LOOKED AT THE DRIVER AND DREAMED OF THE DAY WHEN THEY WOULD BE IN COMMAND OF SUCH A MECHANICAL MONSTER . . . THESE EARLY-DAY TRUCKERS, LIKE THE COWBOYS BEFORE THEM, CAME TO BELIEVE THE MYTHS ABOUT THEMSELVES.

The experimentation with the truck during World War I, the rise of interstate trucking at the time of the Great Depression, the success of the truck during World War II, and the interstate highway boom following the war all fueled a new, seminomadic way of life. The

This 1969 picture illustrates three makes of trucks that were operated by California Industrial Products of Santa Fe Springs, California. Seen here from left to right are a Peterbilt conventional, a Kenworth cab-over, and an RL700 Mack conventional.

Truck Market Shares

Class 8 Market Shares	1997	1998	
	%	%	
1. Freightliner	28.2	31.2	64,307
2. Navistar	19.3	18.7	38,583
3. Mack	12.5	13.0	26,801
4. Volvo	9.7	11.7	24,064
5. Kenworth	10.1	10.8	22,347
6. Peterbilt	11.3	10.3	21,168
7. Sterling	N/A	2.5	5,055
8. Western Star	1.4	1.5	3,017
9. Other	0.5	0.4	878
10. Ford	7.0	0.0	0

Note: Class 8 truck sales were 206,220 in 1998, an increase of 27,669 from the previous year, and up from just under 150,000 a decade earlier. Class 8 trucks sales dipped to a low point of just under 100,000 during the economic slump of 1991. The 1998 market shares are adjusted to total 100 percent.

(**Sources:** *Commercial Carrier Journal*, March 1999; *Trucking Technology*, May/June 1998)

invention and innovation of trucks during the past half-century helped keep trucking front-and-center in the American economy. Today, we continue to marvel at the grace and power of semi-trucks. Today's sleek styling creates the impression that cargo is being floated along our roads. While Americans see big rigs on a daily basis and frequently encounter drivers, most know little about the semi-truck. Its invention, development, and refinement is a story that will be told here through words and photographs. We follow Henry Ford's simple philosophy: "I think that unless we know more about machines and their use, unless we better understand the mechanical portion of life, we cannot have time to enjoy the trees, and the birds, and the flowers, and the green fields."

SEMI-TRUCK BASICS

The semi-truck is typically divided into two parts: a tractor pulls at least one trailer. This book details the many makes of tractors. While tractors are produced by a variety of manufacturers, they have a lot in common. All tractors are driven by an engine, and they all have a cab where the driver sits. The design of tractors, as we will see, can be understood from the historical forces that created the American semi-truck in the early part of the twentieth century.

The movement away from horse-drawn carriages and toward motor cars set the stage for the development of trucks and trucking. At first, automobiles were a novelty. But it soon became obvious, especially with the scarcity and costs associated with maintaining horses, that trucks would have commercial applications. There was a hitch. The nation needed to build a system of roads. Roads provided a new freedom from the rail-driven economy. And by the 1950s, the development of an expansive interstate highway system in the United States allowed the nation to take advantage of its unique and vast natural resources.

In this book we will speak of "semis" because most tractors pull a semi-trailer that has only rear wheels hitched to a fifth wheel—a circular hinged plate at the rear of the tractor. The trailer bolt that fits into the fifth wheel enables it to turn corners and maneuver. Most American semi-trailers have been called "eighteen wheelers"—the tractor has a total of 10 wheels, and most trailers have 8. Except for the front wheels of the tractor, most wheels are duals. Semis are designed with handling in mind. In contrast to the automobile, tractors feature oversized sideview mirrors, air brakes, manual and more complex transmission-clutch systems, and plenty of room. Snubnose cab-over and conventional long nose trucks burn diesel fuel vented through exhaust stacks. The finest trucks are "sleepers" which feature a bunk for two in the rear of the cab.

THE TRUCK CULTURE

Trucks and trucking have a unique spot in American culture. Some have contended that truck drivers are America's modern cowboys. According to author James Thomas:

> THE APPALOOSA STALLION AND THE SIX-GUN WERE SYMBOLS OF POWER FOR THE COWBOY; IN MORE RECENT TIMES, A DIESEL-POWERED KENWORTH IS THE TRUCKER'S STEED, AND COMMAND OF A 60,000-POUND CARGO WRAPPED IN CHROME AND STEEL IS THE TRUCKER'S POWER SYMBOL. COURAGE IS NECESSARY TO CONTROL SUCH AWESOME POWER TO TURN A STAMPEDING HERD OR TO RIDE TO THE BOTTOM OF A MOUNTAIN ROAD WHEN THE BRAKES FAIL.

The trucking "mystique" has been driven by popular culture. From Humphrey Bogart's performance in *They Drive by Night* to Dennis Weaver's victimization in *Duel*, truckers have been portrayed as feared by automobile drivers. Perhaps this is why the nation became attracted to larger and larger Sport Utility Vehicles (SUVs) and pickup trucks to battle for position on the highway. At the same time, the trucker is a symbol of independence. Through such movies as *White Line Fever* and television news reporting of trucking, truckers have been portrayed as what sociologist Herbert Gans has labeled "rugged individualists"—willing to buck the establishment and push the limits of law. The reality of trucks and trucking today is, of course, more subdued.

THE TRUCKING THREAD

In this book, we will trace the world of trucks and trucking to its roots in agriculture and industrialization. Trucks came of age during two world wars, proving themselves to be efficient defenders of the American democratic model. At the same time, the development of trucks is a story of innovation and constant change. While trucks and trucking were a constant throughout the last century, they survived because of a steady stream of re-engineering.

Today, truck manufacturing has moved from a scattered collection of hundreds of machine-shop experimenters to a global network of just a few huge multinational corporations

that control the lion's share of the market. By the beginning of the twenty-first century, Freightliner, Navistar, Mack, Kenworth, and Peterbilt were among the nameplates producing and selling thousands of trucks each year. And Volvo, Sterling, and Western Star had made their moves in the highly competitive Class 8 semi-truck industry. Automobile manufacturers such as Ford, GMC, Chevrolet, and Dodge had taken a back seat, focusing on lighter-weight trucks. International partnerships such as DaimlerChrysler recast the industry in a new global light. The future looked bright for those with the toughness to earn reputations as builders of quality trucks.

In the next chapter, we will examine the history of semi-trucks in America and set the stage to view manufacturers such as Mack, Freightliner, Kenworth, Peterbilt, International, White, GMC, Ford, Dodge, Diamond T, and Marmon. Also, we'll look at some of the nameplates of the past that are "gone but not forgotten." And, we'll look ahead to the new century with its emphasis on trucks manufactured by global corporate giants. So, hop aboard and prepare to put the pedal to the metal! Come along as we travel the roads of trucks that are here for the long haul, as well as those that are gone. With the help of photographer Stan Holtzman, we will marvel at the evolution of the American semi. By the end of our journey, you might see the trucks on the road today in a different light. You will come to respect the beauty and majesty of the awesome big rigs that carry America's load.

Truckers are individuals who "walk to the beat of their own drum." They cannot be confined to a small 5x8-foot office space, running a computer, with some clever phrase or family pictures adorning their cubicle. The little plastic figure atop the hood of this T600 Kenworth is a tribute to truckers' individualism. They are free spirits, and though they may not have a 401K plan and they make less money than those working for big government or big corporations, truckers are a resource that cannot be overlooked.

CHAPTER 1

HISTORY

As early as the 1830s, self-propelled carriages . . . were powered by steam boilers
which required inordinate amounts of fuel and water,
and they had the unsettling tendency to explode.

—James H. Thomas (1979)

In Europe, the earliest attempts to move carriages with something other than horsepower fueled public fear. People worried that the human body could not survive speeds faster than 30 miles per hour and thought that breathing would stop in such wind. It took most of the nineteenth century for people to abandon such notions and to find reliable fuel sources. In 1884 in Germany, Gottlieb Daimler patented his internal combustion engine, which was soon used to power a horseless carriage. Many worked on the invention, but Daimler and another German, Carl Benz, are credited as the pioneers.

In America by this time a host of inventors began using gasoline-powered engines in their automobile designs. By the 1890s, trucks began to appear. Alexander Winton and the White Sewing Machine Company of Cleveland were among those testing all forms of power: steam, gasoline, and even batteries. The first trucks were built by White from used touring cars, but the interest from the business community quickly led to the building and selling of new trucks. However, truck size was limited because, up until the early part of the twentieth century, designers built trucks out of used automobile frames.

Despite interest in motorized transportation at the turn of the century, it was not yet clear that a truck would be cheaper to operate than horses people already owned. In 1903, the public still had to be sold on the idea that trucks were more efficient than horses, so the Automobile Club of America sponsored a test in New York City. Eleven companies ran trucks of various weights along the 20-mile course. Truck historian James Thomas reported that "the giant of the field was a steam-powered Courtland from Preston, England, which carried 12,000 pounds and boasted 30 horsepower." He concluded that the two-day event proved that gasoline engines were the most efficient, but the public clung to its huge investment in horse-drawn carriages and continued to decry the "devil's wagons." Trucks were less expensive than horses, and they were better at withstanding extreme temperatures. Still, if a farmer or merchant had horses, he continued to use them. In the years leading up to World War I horses still outnumbered trucks 400 to every 1 of the some 25,000 trucks estimated to be in use.

The military found that men and supplies could be transported hundreds of miles where there were no rail lines, but the young trucking industry had no standards and thousands of designs. After trucks were used in the war in Mexico in 1916 and then in Europe during World War I, the trucking industry could not provide vehicles fast enough to keep pace with demand. As we will see later in this book,

A Kenworth, circa 1963, is seen here in 1970, pulling a mixed set of doubles north on Interstate 5.

Regulation and Deregulation of Trucking

Over the years, the federal government has promoted, regulated, and deregulated trucking. The Interstate Commerce Act of 1887 established the principle of reasonable rates and the idea that an independent body, the Interstate Commerce Commission (ICC), could provide oversight over railroads. The Federal Road Aid Act of 1916 promoted trucking by providing federal road funding. Between 1919 and 1929, states adopted gasoline taxes. By 1925, 35 states had trucking safety, service, and pricing regulations. By the 1930s, the truck had functionally replaced the horse and wagon. In many ports, traditional rail shipping was shifted to truck hauling within a few short years. Interstate trucking was becoming more common, and railroad revenues plummeted during the Great Depression. There were calls for the federal regulation of interstate trucking. After a failed attempt at self-regulation in 1934, Congress passed the Motor Carrier Act of 1935 giving the ICC broad powers over interstate trucking. Still, as late as 1940, the lion's share of trucking was intrastate, and state regulation was considered burdensome. The Transportation Act of 1940 attempted to deal comprehensively with all types of hauling. The Reed-Bulwinkle Act of 1948 exempted rate cartels from antitrust laws, and this governed trucking for 25 years. ICC regulation between 1935 and 1980 appeared to favor the growth of trucking at the expense of the railroads, and the rules seemed to favor LTL (less-than-truckload) carriers over others within the industry. Particular owners and the Teamsters Union benefited greatly from this scheme. By the 1970s, however, economic analyses demonstrated the growth potential of deregulating trucking. The Motor Carrier Act of 1980 relaxed barriers to entry into the industry and continued the relaxed regulations of the 1970s. Common carriers could now adjust rates to market conditions as much as 10 percent without ICC interference. Deregulation led to a sharp rise in the number of new carriers, consolidation of LTL trucking, and lowered operating costs. The Negotiated Rates Act of 1993 continued the trend of government oversight of industry excesses. And the demise of the Interstate Commerce Commission left the Department of Transportation, other federal agencies, and state regulatory bodies with an increasingly deregulatory view of trucking. Rates and safety issues continued to dominate the regulatory agenda. The Motor Carrier Safety Act of 1999 placed safety issues front-and-center in the hands of a new National Motor Carrier Administration. "The responsible trucking companies and professional truck drivers we represent strongly support the intent of this legislation," said American Trucking Associations' president Walter McCormick. At the same time, the Transportation Equity Act for the Twenty-first Century funded the largest number of highway construction and repair projects since the creation of the interstate highway system in the 1950s. Said McCormick: "The highway is our workplace, so the safety and engineering improvements made possible have special significance for the trucking industry. It also guarantees that, for the first time, taxes paid by highway users—especially trucking companies—will fund the transportation needs of those users and not be drained off for non-related projects."

(**Sources:** Paul Teske, Samuel Best, and Michael Mintrom. 1995. *Deregulating Freight Transportation: Delivering the Goods*. Washington, DC: AEI Press, pp. 25, 27-35, 56-91; and the American Trucking Associations website at http://www.truckline.com.)

most of today's major manufacturers benefited greatly from both world wars where they were able to prove their value to the nation.

The war also benefited the truck industry in another way. A half-million horses were sent to Europe during the war, and the cost for horses back home skyrocketed. At war's end, surplus trucks and experienced truck drivers came home to a nation that had seen truck production increase tenfold during the war years. The usefulness of trucks was still limited by the problems associated with poor and unpaved roads, but during the 1920s, federal funding for road construction helped change that. The Federal Highway Act of 1921 promoted intercounty and interstate road work. The 1920s also brought windshields, manual wipers, and enclosed truck cabs. In the 1930s, driver comfort was emphasized and manufacturers added padded seats and heaters. These were also important years for improvements in tires, brakes, steering, and suspension. By the time the United States entered World War II, the use of sleeper cabs for cross-country driving was accepted. This was also a time of great shakeout in the young truck industry as the number of manufacturers declined sharply from hundreds to a small group of major players. Auto companies such as Ford and Dodge dominated light truck sales. The heavy truck industry was now made up of well-known nameplates: Mack, White, Diamond Reo, Kenworth, Peterbilt, and International Harvester.

THE MEN AND THEIR VEHICLES: A BRIEF HISTORY OF TRUCKING

The history of trucks in America shifted from large numbers of independent inventors working in small shops to the domination of a handful of large, multinational corporations. The major truck brands today—Mack, Freightliner, Navistar, Kenworth, Peterbilt—have much in common. They all survived by taking advantage of circumstances, such as world wars, and by exploiting these opportunities. They all continued to be innovative in truck design, and their willingness to develop new features moved the industry forward and guaranteed their place in history.

THE MEN AND THEIR MOTOR VEHICLES

Cyrus McCormick saw his father try and fail to build a mechanical grain reaper in the early 1800s. Our story of trucking really begins with his dreams and persistence. The McCormicks' Virginia farm test grounds, and the 1846 opening of a production plant in Chicago, marked the beginning of the social shift from horse to machine.

The men who promoted the efficiency of machine power came from all backgrounds. Thomas Howard White was part of a group that founded a Massachusetts sewing machine plant in 1859. There were no motor-driven carriages in 1875 when Walter Chrysler was born in Kansas. The son of a passenger railroad engineer, young Walter "loved to ride over the plains beside his father in the cab of the snorting iron juggernaut." He thought he would follow his father's footsteps in the railroad business. As the nineteenth century entered its last decade, the entrepreneurial spirit was alive. Motor-driven vehicles were new technology, and everybody wanted to get on board.

In 1890, Jack Mack landed a job at the carriage and wagon firm of Fallesen & Berry in Brooklyn, New York. Just two years later, in Springfield, Massachusetts, other inventors built the first successful gasoline motor engine–powered car. By 1893, Jack and brother Gus Mack had purchased a factory. The Mack brothers had managed to repair foreign automobiles and began experimenting with their own design for motorized wagons. Still others tried their hands at designing.

Jonathon Dixon Maxwell, one of the true pioneers of the industry, had collaborated with Elwood Haynes in building the first Haynes car in 1894. By 1899 work began on the Maxwell automobile. Henry Ford designed his first truck that same year, six years after work was completed on an experimental car. The automobile was still seen as a novelty with no commercial potential. So, investors in the Detroit Auto Company sought for three years to sell each car for "the largest possible price." That venture eventually became Cadillac. Ford later wrote, "I found that the new company was not a vehicle for realizing my ideas but merely a money-making concern—that did not make much money." Henry Ford formed his own company that would implement his philosophy of building quality-made, yet inexpensive, vehicles.

Frank and William Fageol foresaw the motorized future in 1899 when they built a car in Iowa that ran on gasoline. In the meantime, Thomas White's three sons developed an interest in cars and trucks. Walter White became president of the White Motor Company, which built two steam-powered pie wagons in 1900.

Like many handy fellows at the dawn of the twentieth century, young Max and Morris Grabowsky were using their Detroit machine shop to fiddle with motor cars. With the backing of Barney Finn and Albert Marx, who operated a popular saloon, the Grabowskys launched what would eventually become the huge General Motors

Corporation. Some time between 1900 and 1902, they sold their first one-cylinder (horizontally mounted) engine truck. At first their venture was named Rapid Motor Vehicle Company, credited with the first American manufacture of cars in quantity in 1901.

That same year, John and Horace Dodge's design and construction skills won them a contract with Oldsmobile. Not to be outdone, Henry Ford offered the Dodge boys a one-tenth share in his new company in exchange for their expertise in building motors and transmissions.

By this time, Jack Mack had a vision: "to produce the most durable and powerful heavy-duty trucks and engines in the world." The Mack brothers introduced their first successful vehicle with a prototype completed and sold in 1902.

Charles A. Tilt began building cars in 1905. One day, a few years later, one of his customers asked him to build a truck for hauling plumbing supplies. Wanting the business, Tilt agreed. Seeing the potential, he launched a line of trucks. The first Diamond T was a conventional four-cylinder one-and-a-half-ton truck. Tilt's father had made Diamond Brand shoes under a green diamond trademark with a gold border and a T inside. The T stood for Tilt.

Brothers Louis and Edgar Gerlinger originally sold cars in Portland, Oregon, and the early models required a lot of maintenance. Gerlinger founding mechanic Ed Hahn told a company publication that their earliest truck was born out of a need to keep busy in a fledgling industry; the repair garage was a necessity in order to

A Look Back at 1973

In 1973, as the Vietnam War ended and "The Morning After" played on American radios across the country, trucking was changing. Ford's L Series trucks were popular, but the auto giant was having trouble keeping pace with dramatic developments. Freightliner's 96-inch cab-over led to booming sales. Within a year, Freightliner debuted its long conventional truck. The Mack V600 ST was considered an industry "workhorse." And Kenworth commemorated its 50th anniversary with a gold background radiator ornament. The

W900 conventional was a popular rig of the period. Trucking during the 1970s would be dominated by fuel shortages and cost concerns. By the end of 1973, truckers were dealing with fuel quotas, a doubling of costs, and a black market. The decade set the stage for major shifts during the 1980s and 1990s.

(**Source:** "Looking back at 1973." *Land Line*, November 1998, pp. 10-13.)

Gasoline is being loaded into an underground fuel tank at a gas station during the fuel crisis of 1974. Sharp price increases in 1999–2000 briefly reminded people of those troubled days.

A 1955 GMC 900 series is exiting a major freeway in Los Angeles.

sell people on the idea of purchasing exciting but unreliable motor cars. When the mechanics were idle and lacking repair work, they continued with their truck-building project. That first truck was called the Gersix, a six-cylinder vehicle built in 1915 out of structural steel that weighed more than two tons.

International used the basic design of the Auto Buggy, attached a small bed to the rear, and produced its first truck in 1909. They called it the Auto Wagon Express, and it was designed to help farmers get produce to market. The first trucks had both air- and water-cooled engines. The truck carried an IHC nameplate, replaced simply by "International" in 1914. By this time, International moved from two-cylinder to four-cylinder engines.

Leland James, the man behind Freightliner, built his first small truck in 1913 to haul sand and gravel around town in Portland, Oregon. Business was good, but he saw a larger opportunity: long hauling. He worked from a "you pay, we'll haul it" business approach that quickly caught on. There was a problem, however: trucks of the day were not designed to travel long distances.

The partnership that Henry Ford had forged in 1902 with the Dodge brothers ended in 1914 when Dodge Brothers incorporated. About this time, Frank and William Fageol moved their garage to California. Fageol Motor Company was founded in 1916 with the financial help of W. H. Bill. Fageol trucks came to be called "Bill-Bilt."

World War I was the first test for the American trucking industry. Wartime production helped convince Americans there was a future for the horseless carriage. Bolstered by a shortage of horses, trucks began to fill the gap.

By 1925, Walter Chrysler had moved from railroads to motor cars, and he formed what would become the Chrysler Corporation under a voluntary plan to transfer Maxwell Motor Corporation stock, valued at $400 million.

As the American labor movement took shape, labor unions such as the Teamsters had a dramatic impact on the form of the young trucking industry. The union movement brought improvements in working conditions and hourly wages.

In 1938, after Sterling Motors Company of Milwaukee had taken over, Sterling wanted Fageol's sales distribution network but sold the manufacturing and assembly plants to T. A. Peterman, a logging entrepreneur from Washington state who wanted to build his own trucks under his Peterman Manufacturing Company. He liked his "Bill-Bilt" Fageols and decided to produce trucks under the "Peterbilt" nameplate. The first Peterbilt trucks used the Fageol egg-crate-style grille, but as production inched up during World War II, Peterbilt trucks took on their modern look. The trucks continued to be manufactured at Fageol's Oakland, California, plant.

While Henry Ford was cranking out hundreds of trucks a day, T. A. Peterman was setting his sights on building one hundred trucks a year, concentrating on quality, not quantity. Factory records state that 14 trucks were actually shipped that partial first year, and the 1940 production total for a whole year was 82 units.

World War II was the testing ground for the modern American semi-truck. The companies able to produce durable, heavy-duty trucks—Mack, Ford, GMC—emerged with a leadership role in the peacetime economy.

The development of efficient interstate highway travel helped secure trucking during the 1950s and 1960s. Economic downturns and fuel shortages in the 1970s and 1980s led to many shakeouts, as weaker companies withered on the vine. At the same time, the declining influence of labor unions, such as the Teamsters, reshaped the industry. Corporate megamergers of the 1990s redefined the industry as controlled by a few giants.

CHAPTER 2

MACK TRUCKS

The ultimate business tool.
—Mack president and CEO Michel Gigou (1999)

The name Mack is synonymous in American culture with large, strong, and solid. Mack is one of the oldest continuous truck manufacturers in North America, which can be attributed to the company's century-long tradition of innovation. When brothers John "Jack" Mack and Augustus "Gus" Mack helped pioneer the new horseless wagon industry in the 1890s, they began a tradition that continues to this day with the Allentown, Pennsylvania, company's Vision line of heavy trucks.

THE MACK ORIGINS:
FOUR BROTHERS AND MANY IDEAS

In 1890, according to company history, Jack Mack landed a job at the carriage and wagon firm of Fallesen & Berry in Brooklyn, New York. By 1893, he and brother Gus had purchased the factory. The Mack brothers went from repairing foreign automobiles to experimenting with their own design for motorized wagons. Within a year, William "Willie" Mack, who had operated a wagon-building plant in Scranton, Pennsylvania, joined his brothers.

Willie, Jack, and Gus Mack came to build large commercial motor vehicles reportedly after Jack's ride on neighbor Theodore Heilbron's two-cylinder Winton automobile. Heilbron was captain of William Randolph Hearst's private yacht, and he lived a block from the original Mack shop in Brooklyn. According to Mack company records:

> THE SUPERIOR PERFORMANCE OF THE NEW WINTON SOON HAD THE TWO AUTOMOBILISTS IN AN ENTHUSIASTIC MOOD. AND IT WAS NOT LONG BEFORE THEIR CONVERSATION CENTERED ON THE FUTURE DEVELOPMENTS OF GASOLINE ENGINES AND MOTOR VEHICLES. CAPTAIN HEILBRON SUGGESTED TO JACK MACK THAT THE ADAPTATION OF A LARGE GASOLINE ENGINE TO A TRUCK OR SIGHTSEEING BUS WOULD BE A GREAT IDEA.

The Mack brothers realized that carriage making soon would be replaced by motorized wagons and began experimenting with steam and electric motor cars. In 1902, they completed and sold their first successful prototype. It was an 18–20-passenger open-bodied bench seat bus designed for sightseeing concessionaires Harris and McGuire, and it operated in Brooklyn's Prospect Park for several years. The bus was originally powered by a 24-horsepower, four-cylinder, horizontally mounted engine, and it was quickly replaced by a 36-horsepower unit and ultimately a 40-horsepower

This 1984 MH Mack truck and trailer roll-off unit owned by G. I. Industries of Simi Valley, California, was the pride of the fleet. At one time, G. I. owned the Los Angeles Mack Truck dealership.

An H61 Mack "Cherrypicker" is seen in this 1965 photo, taken at Mike & Vic's Truck Stop in North Lima, Ohio. Ol' Yaller was brown and yellow.

vertical engine that reached a top speed of 20 miles per hour but averaged about 12 miles per hour. The vehicle traveled over one million miles. "Old No. 1," as it was called, initiated a history of durable trucks. After eight years of service as a bus, it was converted to a truck. Mack later used a slogan in bus advertisements, "The first Mack was a bus and the first bus was a Mack."

A second bus was ordered in 1903, and from 1904 to 1910 Mack sightseeing vehicles went by the name "Manhattan," probably to distinguish them from the company's horse-drawn wagons. The buses could be found in New York, Boston, New Orleans, and Havana. Between 1902 and 1905, the Mack brothers produced and sold their first 15 buses in Brooklyn before buying a plant in Allentown, Pennsylvania. The Mack Brothers Manufacturing Plant in Brooklyn continued to build wagons and repair automobiles, while the Mack Brothers Motor Car Company was incorporated in Lehigh County, Pennsylvania, to develop and manufacture Mack Trucks.

Metallic blue and white were the colors of this clean LT Mack in 1969. Connolly Transportation of Vernon, California, hauled Hamms beer from the Mexican border to the Oregon border in this sharp rig.

An extralong concrete beam takes on a new dimension when this LT Mack does the pulling. Progressive Transportation of Compton, California, had a fleet of LT Macks as well as older Peterbilts.

With Mack buses growing in popularity, the three brothers joined youngest Mack sibling, Joseph, in purchasing the second plant in Allentown. Joe owned a silk mill in Allentown, and he became Mack company treasurer following the move in 1905. It was at this point that the Mack brothers tested and marketed their first truck. They offered customers a four-cylinder, 60-horsepower basic engine, and a more husky six-cylinder 90-horsepower model. A five-ton Senior line vehicle was available by 1908, joined by 1–2-ton Junior line vehicles in 1909. The Mack brothers' experience with the Manhattan tour bus, hotel buses, and other passenger vehicles had positioned them to compete in the emerging truck market.

Mack became one of the first manufacturers to mount a cab directly over the engine. This feature increased driver visibility and maneuverability, an important safety feature on crowded city streets. The "Manhattan" cab-over-engine model helped define the new company by 1905 and was the forerunner of the modern cab-over-engine (COE) trucks. Jack Mack, in the meantime, patented immediate shifting between high to low gears for maximum efficiency on hilly terrain. Gus Mack's patented constant-mesh selective gearbox protected gears from being damaged or stripped by inexperienced drivers.

Moving a little ahead of ourselves, we see this Mack Superliner, brightly painted and looking like a typical New England truck. This beauty is owned by Bentley Warren of Ipswich, Massachusetts. The photo was taken in 1988.

An RS600 Mack ready-mix truck is seen on the job in Las Vegas, Nevada, and is one of several units owned by Abco Ready Mix Sand & Gravel.

The Mack brothers were leaders in the first truck drive, diesel-electric rail cars, design of gear-grinding machines, and Mack chain-drive rear axles when they built America's first motorized hook and ladder fire truck for the city of Morristown, New Jersey, in 1910. The next year, they delivered America's first engine-driven fire pumper truck to Cynwyd, Pennsylvania. It is important to note that through 1910, Mack production was what *The Complete Encyclopedia of Commercial Vehicles* called "modest"–fewer than 100 vehicles each year. It was at this point that the "Manhattan" trade name was dropped, and trucks first were stamped with the "Mack" nameplate.

At the same time, the Manhattan Motor Truck Company was incorporated by the Mack brothers in Massachusetts to operate several dealerships in that state. Production of trucks increased dramatically to more than 600 units per year.

By the fall of 1911 a holding company named the International Motor Company was formed by the Mack brothers and backed by Wall Street banking giant J. P. Morgan to raise capital for Mack and two other lines. Mack was building a wide range of truck sizes—the largest vehicle weighed more than seven tons. The deal paved the way for the Mack brothers to leave the company so they could go their separate

This picture, taken south of Toledo, Ohio, in 1965 shows an LJ Mack with a 1952 vintage integral sleeper, with an LT hood, radiator, and front fenders. A Cummins 505 Industrial engine is under the hood of this rig. J & L Produce of Haines City, Florida, operated this tractor, and Leonard Davis of Bluefield, West Virginia, was the owner of this Mack.

"Widow Maker" is an H63 Mack circa 1956. This picture was taken at Mike & Vic's Truck Stop near Toledo, Ohio, in 1965.

ways. Gus and Joe left the motor vehicle business. Jack formed Mac-Carr, later renamed Maccar, and built trucks until 1935. Willie stayed on with Mack but also built trucks under a separate line named Metropolitan Motors. Ironically, Mack Truck's visionary founder, Jack Mack, died in a motor car accident 22 years after he took a ride in Theodore Heilbron's 1902 Winton:

IN THE EARLY AFTERNOON OF MARCH 14, 1924, JACK MACK WAS ENROUTE TO A BUSINESS MEETING IN WEATHERLY, PENNSYLVANIA, IN HIS CHANDLER COUPE WHEN HIS LIFE ENDED BEHIND THE WHEEL. HIS CAR BECAME INVOLVED IN AN ACCIDENT WITH A TROLLEY CAR OF THE LEHIGH VALLEY TRANSIT COMPANY, WHICH WAS CROSSING THE ROAD DIAGONALLY. JACK WAS KILLED ALMOST INSTANTLY WHEN HIS LIGHT CAR, BEING PUSHED OFF THE ROAD AHEAD OF THE TROLLEY, WAS CAUGHT AGAINST A HEAVY POLE AND CRUSHED LIKE AN EGG SHELL. HIS BODY WAS INTERRED IN FAIRVIEW CEMETERY IN ALLENTOWN, JUST ABOVE THE FORMER MACK PLANT ON 10TH STREET.

Long before Jack Mack's death, and the exodus of the Mack brothers, new engineers had begun to change the face of the truck company. A decade earlier, Mack Trucks had already begun to forge a reputation built upon the foundation of the four brothers. Between 1911 and 1914 the company experimented with lightweight trucks, but Mack Truck's future was to be determined by a new face and new ideas.

Pat Thomas leased this 1953 W Model Mack to Allan Arthur, for hauling cattle into Nevada, California, and Arizona. He later leased this truck and trailer to Arnold Fairbank Cattle Company of Brawley, California.

23

A 1996 CH Model Mack is seen here at a metal recycling facility in Phoenix, Arizona. This truck is set up as a roll-off operation.

Mass Marketing Mack Trucks: Birth of the Bulldog

Edward Hewitt, an experienced truck designer, became chief engineer at Mack Trucks in 1914 and designed the AB model. More the 50,000 ABs, a replacement for the Junior line, sold in the two decades they were produced. But it was Hewitt's AC model, a heavy-duty truck first built in 1916, that was soon labeled "Bulldog" by British Army engineers. More than 40,000 of the 75-horsepower trucks were manufactured in just 20 years. The truck featured a hood and dash-board-mounted radiator, chain drive, and pressed-steel frame. According to the company:

> Many British military trucks were built by Mack, and one Mack AC truck was built as a military armored car for the New York National Guard. Many more of this famous model were purchased by the U.S. Army. Adopted as the standard 5-ton truck, 4,470 Mack AC trucks went to France with American doughboys . . . The AC Mack truck, with its blunt, bulldog-like snub-nose bonnet, became a rugged durable performer on the battlefields of Europe. Tenacious, it took all the abuse of the roughest terrain and came back for more. When a lesser truck became stuck, the British "Tommies" would yell, "Aye, bring one of those Bulldogs in!" The ACs resembled Bulldogs not only in performance but also in appearance, and hence became known as "the Bulldog Macks."

Because of the success of the Bulldog in the war effort the company changed its name to the Mack-International Motor Truck Corporation. Following World War I, the company continued to be an innovator. Some of the highlights during this period included the following:

1916–Mack originated front axle tapered kingpins with a self-tightening design.
1918–Mack became the first truck manufacturer to use air cleaners and oil filters in trucks to improve fuel efficiency and encourage maintenance savings.
1920–Mack developed the first power truck brakes using a vacuum booster system. At the same time, Mack patented rubber isolator shock absorbers.

In this 1989 picture, we see an MR Mack with a Stagg refuse body. Because of its low-entry cab, the MR Mack is popular in the refuse and recycling industry. The U.S. Postal Service recently took delivery of several hundred of these Macks for mail delivery.

24

G & G Logging of Fairfield, Idaho, owns this sharp B77 Mack. This is a working truck and it turns heads wherever it goes.

1926–Mack designed the first aluminum cylinder truck heads.
1927–Mack was one of the first companies to experiment with high-speed diesel truck engines.
1931–Mack introduced power steering and four-wheel brakes.
1938–Mack introduced its first diesel truck engine.
1939–Mack pioneered a 10-speed transmission.

The 1920s and 1930s had redefined Mack and helped solidify its image. In 1922, the parent company name International Motor Truck Corporation was changed to Mack Trucks, Incorporated, because of confusion with the International Harvester Company. Mack adopted the Bulldog as its corporate symbol and in 1921 began affixing a sheet-metal plate to each side of the cab, showing a bulldog chewing up a book entitled *Hauling Costs*, with "Mack" on his collar, and International Motor Co. of New York. According to the company history, the emblem that is used today was developed in the early 1930s by a recuperating engineer:

EARLY IN 1932, ALFRED FELLOWS MASURY, MACK'S CHIEF ENGINEER, WAS ADMITTED TO THE HOSPITAL FOR AN OPERATION. MASURY WAS ONE OF THOSE INDIVIDUALS WHO WASN'T USED TO HIS HANDS BEING IDLE FOR ANY PERIOD OF TIME. DURING HIS RECUPERATION IN THE HOSPITAL, MASURY DECIDED TO CARVE A BULLDOG . . .

WHETHER THE FIRST BULLDOG HOOD ORNAMENT WAS SOAP OR WOOD, WE DO NOT KNOW...BUT, SHORTLY AFTER HIS RELEASE FROM THE HOSPITAL, HE DID IN FACT CARVE A BULLDOG IN WOOD . . . MASURY APPLIED FOR AND RECEIVED A PATENT FOR HIS DESIGN; THAT BULLDOG DESIGN HAS ADORNED MACK TRUCKS EVER SINCE!

The Mack BJ and BB models, introduced in 1927, were developed in response to the demand for larger capacity and higher speeds. It was at this time that American semi-trucks were coming of age, and Mack would be a player. From 1929 until 1944, Mack reports that they produced 2,601 semi- or full trailers.

FULL TRAILERS WERE OF TWO STYLES, NONREVERSIBLE OR REVERSIBLE. NONREVERSIBLE TRAILERS HAD A SOLIDLY FASTENED REAR AXLE ARRANGEMENT WITH A DRAW BAR ON THE FRONT END SO THAT THE TRAILER COULD BE DRAWN IN ONE DIRECTION. A REVERSIBLE TRAILER HAD AXLE ARRANGEMENTS SIMILAR AT EACH END. EITHER END COULD BE FASTENED IN A STATIONARY POSITION WHILE THE DRAW BAR COULD BE FASTENED TO THE OTHER END OF THE TRAILER. IN THIS WAY, EITHER END COULD BE THE FRONT OF THE UNIT.

Truck Air Transfer runs a fleet of these CH Model Macks. This unit is seen at LAX (Los Angeles International Airport) in 1996.

trucks in the 1950s and introducing new transmissions and rear ends, Mack catapulted into a leadership position in the truck manufacturing industry.

In 1953 Mack introduced the W Model cab-over, and production continued through 1958 with both sleeper and nonsleeper versions. The W Model competed with Kenworth's "Bullnose" and Peterbilt, Freightliner, and White's "Bubblenose" trucks.

But it was the B Model that became the most successful in the Mack line. Mack produced 127,000 B Models, including a whopping 47,459 Model B61s. In the words of the company:

THE B SERIES, INTRODUCED IN 1953, WAS SURELY ONE OF MACK'S MOST SUCCESSFUL AND POPULAR PRODUCTS. ITS PLEASING, ROUNDED APPEARANCE SET A NEW STYLING STANDARD FOR TRUCKS, AS DID THE WIDE RANGE OF MODEL VARIATIONS OFFERED. THERE ARE B MODELS STILL IN ACTIVE SERVICE TODAY, PART OF THE 127,786 BUILT THROUGH 1965. THE YEAR 1953 ALSO MARKED THE INTRODUCTION OF THE FAMOUS THERMODYNE OPEN CHAMBER, DIRECT-INJECTION DIESEL ENGINE, WHICH ESTABLISHED MACK'S TRADITION OF LEADERSHIP IN DIESEL PERFORMANCE AND FUEL EFFICIENCY.

In the late 1980s, Mack Trucks came out with a limited number of Liberty Edition trucks. Pictured here is a 1988 Superliner Liberty Edition, leased to North American Van Lines.

Mack trucks took their reputation of dependability into and out of World War II. More than 4,000 AC Model Bulldogs saw action. The L Model conventional truck with clean styling was also very popular during this period, and 35,000 of these heavy-duty trucks were built between 1940–1956. Some L models had aluminum components with powerful engines to satisfy the long-distance hauling needs of West Coast operators. The LT Mack was a massive truck manufactured after the war and has been called "The Duesenberg of Diesels." It featured single headlights, a large chrome bumper, a longer hood, a mesh grille and, of course, a Bulldog hood ornament.

THE MACK AMERICAN SEMI-TRUCK

After the war, the American semi-truck became the preferred method of transporting goods across a vast nation, and Mack responded with new models and features that would take advantage of the new interstate highway system. By producing a variety of

By 1958 Mack had made subtle changes in the H Model, such as the addition of dual headlights and the lowering of the cab, while still retaining the basic looks of the H61 model.

The H Model, beginning with the H60 "Cherry Picker" also introduced in 1953, was mighty tall but was only produced for four years. The H61 also featured a "Cherry Picker" high ride. These were followed by lower-riding H62 and H63 models built through the 1950s. The early H Model trucks featured single headlights mounted on front fenders, but the H67 added dual headlights and still had a tall look. The H series had very high cabs that were designed with a short bumper-to-back cab dimension to accommodate 35-foot trailers and 45-foot overall legal limits. Mack also produced the G series. It featured an all-aluminum cab for light weight and the ability to haul big payloads, especially in West Coast applications.

In 1956 Mack added to its stable by acquiring the Brockway Motor Company. Brockway began in 1851 with a carriage factory in Homer, New York. Founder William Brockway's son George organized the Brockway Motor Truck Company in 1912 in Cortland, New York, to move the firm into the developing horseless carriage business. The original motor wagons featured simple three-cylinder engines. Following wartime production, Brockway acquired the Indiana Truck Corporation at Marion but later sold it to White Motor Company in the depths of the Great Depression. Like Mack,

An R Model is seen here in Puerto Rico, which became home to many older Macks and Brockways. This picture was taken near San Juan in 1986.

Brockway emerged from World War II with a splendid production record. Its 260 series of heavy-duty trucks was popular. Brockway was a low-volume producer of custom engineered trucks, in contrast to Mack's high-volume approach. In 1958 the Husky mascot appeared on Brockway truck radiators. A wide range of models was produced until the division was closed in 1977–a victim of economic recession.

Mack, meanwhile, had grown in the 1950s by winning a major Army contract, opening a new plant in Hayward, California, and producing the F Model cab-over. The F Model was produced on both coasts until 1982. Mack sold 210,000 conventional R Model trucks between 1965 and 1987. By 1980 Mack was producing its WL and WS models only at Allentown.

The Mack Super Liner, of which 12,000 were produced between 1977 and 1988 at the Hayward plant, featured longer hoods. The

Here we see an LJ Mack with an integral sleeper. Integral sleepers are nothing new; they were available in the late 1920s and early 1930s.

In the late 1960s Mack introduced the MB Model, which was popular for local hauling. The MB had many applications, including refuse hauling and local cartage. Pictured here is an MB Mack pulling a set of containers at the Port of Long Beach, California, for Great Western Container Haulers.

In the late 1950s, Mack came out with the G Model and it was quite popular in both the West and Midwest. Outside door handles were located at the bottom of the doors for easier entry.

"Liberty Edition," with its Statue of Liberty decal, was a particularly impressive truck of the period. Production of the Super Liner conventional heavy hauler ended in 1993.

By 1967 Mack Trucks, Inc., had become a member of the Los Angeles–based Signal Oil and Gas Company. An engine introduced that year by Mack:

> . . . PROVIDED BETTER MAXIMUM HORSEPOWER OVER A WIDER RANGE OF ENGINE SPEEDS THAN ANY OTHER STANDARD DIESEL ENGINE OF ITS DAY. THE ENGINE'S DESIGN LEVELED THE HORSEPOWER CURVE AND, AS A RESULT, INCREASED FUEL EFFICIENCY AND SIGNIFICANTLY REDUCED THE NEED FOR SHIFTING. IT WAS SUCH AN IMPROVEMENT THAT A TRANSMISSION WITH FIVE SPEEDS, RATHER THAN TEN OR MORE, COULD BE USED FOR MOST OVER-THE-ROAD APPLICATIONS. THE . . . TRANSMISSION (TRL 107 SERIES), CREATED IN 1967, WAS THE FIRST TRIPLE COUNTERSHAFT, COMPACT-LENGTH DESIGN FOR CLASS 8 TRUCKS, FEATURING THE HIGHEST TORQUE CAPACITY IN THE INDUSTRY.

In 1969 Mack patented cab air suspension and was the first heavy-duty diesel engine manufacturer to produce its own engine compression brake in 1971. The new Mack World Headquarters opened in Allentown, Pennsylvania, that same year.

The Cruise-Liner (1975–1983) was one of Mack's top cab-over offerings, along with the MB Model of the 1960s and 1970s. The MC/MR series was introduced in 1978. This series featured increased maneuverability and visibility for use in tight city settings.

The Mack CH line, popular for highway applications in the 1990s, was pure Bulldog with its firm styling, broad bumper, squared front, and square headlights. It was introduced in 1988. About the same time, Mack introduced the MH Ultra-Liner model with the first "all-fiberglass, metal cage-reinforced cab." In 1987 the commercial vehicle division of Renault—Renault V. I.—bought out the Mack shares from its parent company. Mack introduced the CH series for highway applications in the late 1980s. In 1990 Mack Trucks, Inc., became a wholly owned subsidiary of Renault V. I.

THE MACK VISION

In 1999, Mack introduced the Vision series, a new premium highway tractor. According to Mack: "Its sleek aerodynamic styling and leading-edge technologies were designed from the ground up to give drivers the power, handling, and comfort they want—without compromising the low operating cost, efficiency, and serviceability demanded by fleet managers in the competitive transportation industry."

Safety Issues and Media Coverage

Debate rages today about the safety record of the American semi-truck. It is fueled by officials' intense scrutiny and media coverage. On the one hand, trucks are often involved in multiple pileups. In 1999, for example, 70 people were injured and 150 vehicles damaged on Interstate 10 south of San Bernardino, California. An Associated Press photograph featured a Freightliner semi across the roadway with two small cars slammed into its side. Authorities blamed a sudden storm, high speeds, and rush-hour traffic.

On the other hand, the American semi-truck rides among the nearly 215 million vehicles on U.S. roads. Despite tremendous growth, the government has reported that traffic deaths per mile have decreased by 90 percent since 1925. Safety measures such as seat belts, soft dashboards, roadway lighting, painted lanes, guardrails, barriers, and other innovations reduced deaths from 18 to just 1.7 per 100 million vehicle miles traveled, according to the Centers for Disease Control's National Center for Injury Prevention and Control. Two-thirds of all drivers now say they wear seat belts, and child safety seats have reduced deaths among our youngest passengers.

An older White-Freightliner cattle truck is seen lying on its side after an accident. A dead cow can be seen inside the body of this rig.

By one estimate, driver fatigue is a factor in as many as 40 percent of heavy truck highway crashes. As many as 1,500 deaths each year may be caused by truck drivers falling asleep at the wheel. While safety advocates blame long hours, irregular work schedules, and pay-per-mile wages, the American Trucking Association counters that the time of day is the largest influence on fatigue. The National Highway Traffic Safety Administration reports that large trucks were involved in 444,000 crashes in 1997. About 133,000 people were injured and 5,355 were killed. However, the U.S. Department of Transportation reported that truck fatalities were down from 1988 when there were 5,679 deaths. The fatality rate declined from 3.5 to 2.4 per 100 million miles traveled. Nevertheless, Maine Senator Olympia Snowe has said: "We need to revise the antiquated rules governing duty and rest hours."

The government has sought to increase funding for enforcement of existing rules, research to make trucks safer, and stiffer penalties for violators. For example, a trucker who disregards rail-crossing warnings would be subject to immediate loss of license and a hefty fine. A proposal in 2000 called for a maximum 12-hour work day, and no more than 10 hours of driving. "They treat us as if we don't know we're tired," driver Dee Raines told the *Omaha World-Herald*. "We'll go to bed when we're tired." Following a 1999 truck-Amtrak crash that killed 11 people, the industry countered that no amount of regulations will guarantee safety. "There will always be some character," said United Motorcoach Association Spokesman Steve Sprague, "who justifies it as a cost of doing business." News magazine, newspaper, and television coverage are likely to continue to focus on the dramatic visual impact provided by deadly truck accidents.

(**Sources:** Associated Press, April 29 & May 14, 1999; *Parade Magazine*, May 16, 1999; *USA Today*, May 26, 1999, and *Omaha World -Herald*, June 25, 2000.)

Backed by international capital and a global vision of the twenty-first century, Mack appears to be a survivor in the ever-shrinking list of companies producing the American semi-truck. But the Renault takeover meant that the uniquely American semi-truck would be replaced by designs targeted at an international marketplace.

This was particularly true following the sale of Renault's RVI truck division, including Mack, to Volvo in early 2000. The $1.6 billion deal, according to CEO Mark Gustafson, "is a marriage built on strength versus weakness." Under the merger, French Renault retains a 15 percent share of Swedish Volvo, a company with surging U. S. sales—up a whopping 93 percent between 1996 and 1999. So, the Mack and Volvo nameplates, as a team, may challenge for leader in truck sales in the new century.

Ol' Blue/USA *relays highway safety messages to both the motoring public and to truckers via the many truck shows that it attends. These two crash dummies help get the point across.*

An LF Mack is seen here unloading a steel structure in the Los Angeles area in 1964.

BELOW: *In this 1970 picture, we see an early MH Mack set up as a truck and trailer, a combination that is fairly common in the West. This load consists of fencing material.*

An F Model Mack, circa 1963, is seen here south of Toledo, Ohio, in 1965. F Model Macks were especially popular with the many "bedbug haulers" of that time, and the 7 Santini Brothers was only one of the many van lines that liked the F Model Mack.

BELOW: *The B Model Mack was one of the most beloved Macks ever produced. Here is a B Model with an integral sleeper in service as a livestock truck in Texarkana, Texas, in 1965.*

The Vision is Mack's latest entry for the new millennium. The Vision brings with it the latest in Mack technology and engineering, yet it is light enough to compete with any of its rivals. This unit is owned by Fimbres Trucking of Apple Valley, California, and is used for hauling powdered cement.

CHAPTER 3

FREIGHTLINER

The twentieth century is as good as over.
Our purpose is to look forward, not behind.

—James L. Hebe, Freightliner president and CEO (1999)

Freightliner is indeed a company that has always looked forward in its design of the American semi-truck. Freightliner started with a simple idea: light is better. It is an approach that took this truck manufacturer from a garage in Portland, Oregon, to the top of truck sales at the end of the twentieth century—30.7 percent of all Class 8 truck sales in 1999.

FREIGHTLINER ORIGINS:
REDESIGNING SEMI-TRUCKS IN THE NORTHWEST

Leland James, the man behind Freightliner, built his first small truck in 1913 to haul sand and gravel around town in Portland. Business was good, but he saw a larger opportunity: long hauling. He worked from a "you pay, we'll haul it" business approach that quickly caught on. There was a problem, however: trucks of the day were not designed to travel long distances. And though the development of the American semi-truck was well underway by the 1930s, it was far from a perfected mode of transport. At Consolidated Freightways (CF), a freight company started by Leland James in 1929, the major concern was how to increase shipping weight payload. The answer, Leland James thought, was to reduce the weight of the truck by using new lightweight aluminum for as much of the truck as possible. The

trucks CF could buy were too heavy, and no existing manufacturer was interested in the plan to use aluminum. So CF set out to build its own truck.

CF began experimenting with parts such as brake shoes, and by 1936, it was making whole truck and trailer bodies out of aluminum. CF mechanics were experimenting and learning that, indeed, you could build a better truck by constructing it from lightweight materials. In 1937, they used a Fageol and a Cummins six-cylinder diesel engine to build the cab-over model CF-100. In 1940, James founded Freightways Manufacturing in Utah to build trucks for companies throughout the American West that wanted to increase payload yet stay within weight limits. In the years 1939–1941, the company built 714 trucks.

FREIGHTLINER OVERVIEW

The first "Freight-Liner," as it was called then, was built in 1940. But the joint venture by CF and other companies drew the ire of the United States Department of Justice almost immediately. The government charged that the cooperative was actually a monopoly and ended the carriers' partnership. Freightliner Corporation emerged from the legal scuffle, and manufacturing was returned to Portland.

A Freightliner Super Tanker is seen here delivering almost 13,000 gallons of gasoline at a Texaco gas station in Las Vegas, Nevada.

A 1947 White-Freightliner is seen here at a truck show in California. This restoration is authentic, right down to the nuts and bolts. This is exactly the way this truck looked when it left the factory in Oregon and was purchased by Consolidated Freightways.

Many truckers that owned White-Freightliners in the early 1950s added a box sleeper, as many of these trucks had day-cabs. This White-Freightliner's picture was taken in 1963 at the old Martinez Truck Stop on Alameda Street in Los Angeles. It ran the West Coast, hauling produce.

The government action, though, forced the company to cease production in 1941, and it did not resume for six years.

Following World War II, Freightliner was identified as a company committed to aluminum construction. Now its challenge was to take the lightweight material and make it stronger for use in Class 8 rigs. The Model 800 "bubblenose" cab-over was introduced in 1947 as an alternative to the conventional Model 600. In the same year the company built a new truck plant in Portland. The cab-over-engine design was very popular. Three years later, Freightliner sold its first Model 900–the very first transcontinental sleeper tractor. In fact, this first Model 900, custom-built for the Hyster Company in Portland, was restored in 1976 and can be seen at the Smithsonian Institution.

In this 1956 photo, we see a White-Freightliner with a birdcage grille unloading cattle at the L.A. Union Stockyards in Vernon, California. This rig had a Cummins 220-horsepower "Pancake" engine under its cab, which was quite popular in trucking during this time. John Shubin, dba Livestock Transport, was based in El Monte, California, and hauled cattle and sheep in California and Arizona, using White-Freightliners, Peterbilts, GMCs, and International trucks.

Back in the 1950s, it was common for truckers to haul livestock to California, unload the critters, steamclean the truck bodies and trailers, and then backhaul either produce or freight. Seen at the wash rack at the L.A. Union Stockyards in 1956, this White-Freightliner is being washed out so it can return to Colorado with a load of produce.

In this 1960 photo, a White-Freightliner is seen running through Indio, California, on its way to Texas. The drom box, behind the cab, allows more freight to be carried. This rig was one of many that ran for Western-Gillette, an outfit that hauled both LTL and TL freight from California to Texas and back.

The use of aluminum meant that Freightliner trucks were more than a ton lighter than conventional rigs. Freightliner had become a pioneer in meeting the design needs of long haulers.

Freightliner continued to develop the cab-over design with the first tilt-over/cab-over in 1958. The size of the sleeper became more spacious during this period. By the late 1960s, Freightliner sleepers were a whopping 107 inches long.

In the 1950s Freightliner moved to the White Freightliner nameplate as part of an exclusive sales and service deal. It was a way for Freightliner to take advantage of White's vast dealer network at that time. White had acquired Sterling in 1951 and had a solid marketing strategy. Between 1951 and 1977 more than 100,000 White Freightliner trucks were sold. Then, Freightliner returned to its original nameplate after the partnership expired. Freightliner had become a popular brand with large carriers such as Werner Enterprises and

A White-Freightliner conventional truck and trailer in 1975. Most of the conventionals simply said Freightliner on them, but the early 1970 models still sported the words White-Freightliner.

Truck Engines

The engines that move American semi-trucks are an important part of our story. Names such as Cummins, Caterpillar, and Detroit Diesel are the driving forces behind the industry.

Truck engine development: A chromed Detroit V-12 Diesel is seen in the late Jerry "Tyrone" Malone's Boss Truck of America in 1970.

Cummins has experienced global growth for more than 80 years and has been a Class 8 truck engine leader in North America for more than a quarter century. Cummins engines such as the Signature 600, ISX, N14 Plus, ISM, ISL, ISC, and ISB feature plenty of horsepower. Cummins also developed SmartTorque technology, which integrates electronic control of the transmission and engine. According to Cummins, "SmartTorque 2 delivers . . . improved hill-climbing performance with less downshifting and less wear and tear on your transmission."

Detroit Diesel is one of the world's leading heavy-duty engine manufacturers with more than 6,000 employees. The company features 500 engine models ranging from 10 to 10,000 horsepower. Detroit Diesel, like Cummins, claims leadership in the Class 8 market in North America: "When using our products, you'll be satisfied with their low cost of ownership, long life to overhaul, reliability, and durability."

Detroit Diesel began in 1938 with the formation of the Detroit Diesel Engine Division by General Motors. After World War II, Detroit Diesel focused on the highway heavy-duty truck engine market. In 1970, General Motors consolidated the Detroit Diesel Engine Division and the Allison Division in Indianapolis to form the Detroit Diesel Allison Division. On January 1, 1988, a joint venture was formed between Penske Corporation and General Motors.

Caterpillar Cat engines are used in on-highway trucks, ships and boats, locomotives, and construction, mining, and agricultural equipment. By 1999, Cat truck engine sales kept this giant profitable. Caterpillar chairman and CEO Glen Barton says: "While sales of large machines remained weak, truck engine sales continued at historic high levels." The Cat C-10 truck engine is featured by the company. Cat focuses on durability and fuel economy: "Fuel economy is a key component of owning and operating costs and the Cat C-10 engine delivers fuel economy performance on par with the industry-leading 3176B truck engine."

Cummins, Detroit Diesel, and Caterpillar remind us to look under the hood for the power of trucks. Design improvements in the future will focus on reliability, maintenance, durability, power, and operating costs.

In the mid-1970s and for only a short time, Freightliner made the Powerliner cab-over. This rig sported a wider radiator and grille area for the more powerful V-12 Detriot Diesels. Hardly anything on this model could interchange into any other model of Freightliner. The windshield was larger, and even the doors were another size. Tom Stone, a trucker from Montana, ran this Powerliner.

Swift Transportation because it was known as a dependable truck. While Freightliner continued to emphasize lightweight truck design, the company offered another new idea: interchangeable parts. Freightliner introduced a conventional model in 1974 that boasted some 80 percent of its parts could be used on its popular cab-over models.

THE NEW STERLING

Freightliner's market share was boosted at the end of the 1990s by its acquisition of the Sterling Truck Corporation and Ford Motor Corporation's remaining stock of heavy trucks. Sterling, "the mark of quality," is viewed as a new line of customized trucks. Freightliner's founding of Sterling in 1998 as a subsidiary marked the dawning of

Longer vehicle combinations, as seen on this Freightliner hauling material outside of Las Vegas, Nevada, at Lone Mountain, mean more payload and more revenue.

Here we see a 1980s Freightliner conventional at a truck show in California. Even though the weather was overcast, the bright colors are quite obvious on both the tractor and trailer.

Center State Transport of Fresno, California, is famous for its pink fleet of Freightliner trucks. Pictured here are two Freightliner models at a truck show.

a new and distinctive era. Sterling is headquartered in Willoughby, Ohio, near Cleveland. Backed by the resources of the world's leading commercial vehicle manufacturer, DaimlerChrysler, Sterling trucks are targeted at the "vocational" market–those truckers doing more than just hauling freight. Sterling trucks feature rugged design and efficient power. Sterling's goal is to become a world-class truck company in the twenty-first century. "Our relationship with Freightliner Corporation–the parent company of Sterling–brings instant credibility to our products," said senior vice president John Merrifield. Sterling launched a parts and service organization, dubbed Alliance, to further its marketing goals. The SilverStar model is the top-of-the-line tractor engineered for independent owners/drivers. The 9500 series is targeted at long haul and offroad uses. The 8500 series offered a wide range of midsize diesels. Transportation Services Incorporated has a fleet of 80 Sterling ST9500 SilverStars. The Sterling SilverStar features a standup aluminum sleeper cab, a choice of Cummins, Caterpillar, or Detroit Diesels engines up to 500 horsepower, and a streamlined look. "Drivers love the truck," said TSI vice president Kenneth Pellegrino. "In fact, they don't want to drive anything else."

Tractors with a very short wheelbase are important for mobile-home truckers, as some of the trailers they tote are extremely long and very wide. For this reason, Rudy & Son, a mobile-home hauler from Utah, chose to truck with this Freightliner.

Freightliner Trucks were one of the very first truck makers to build with aluminum. Lighter-weight trucks meant hauling more payload, and that's especially important for haulers like Valley Livestock Transportation of Dixon, California. Valley has been hauling cattle and sheep in the West for over 50 years.

Sterling is a customer-oriented truck company that has earned the respect of its clients. "We need a very maneuverable truck with great visibility," George E. Fern Company's Louisville manager Jeff Hall told Sterling. Grane Transportation Industries' Herbert "Bud" Grane, Jr., added this about the company's 16 Sterling A9500s: "It is a good product that fits the needs of the Chicago area very well . . . a tractor that has maneuverability to handle tight city conditions, while still having the comfort." In Alaska, World Wide Movers' Pete Sorenson likes the way Sterling's 460 horsepower Cummins diesel configuration handles the rough arctic terrain: "Our trucks go to some ugly parts of the state, but that is where the customer is and you go take care of him." The power and comfort are popular with his drivers. "They are quiet, they have great ride, they are comfortable, and they have big, roomy cabs," Sorenson added. "They told me they are blowing past all the other trucks on the uphills." Sterling trucks are sold in the United States, Canada, Australia, New Zealand, and Mexico. They are manufactured in St. Thomas, Ontario. Sterling, taking advantage of its corporate partnership, finances new rigs through Mercedes-Benz Credit Corporation.

The Freightliner Legacy series is a popular model for local cartage. Seen leaving the Hughes warehouse in Irwindale, California, a Legacy delivers groceries to one of the many Hughes facilities in Los Angeles. Hughes was taken over by a larger conglomerate, but when it was in business, Hughes had a fleet of these Legacy Freightliners.

A HOT FREIGHTLINER FUTURE

In 1981, when Daimler-Benz (as it was then called) purchased Freightliner, truck sales continued to soar for the global giant. Freightliner ended the century with a solid reputation for manufacturing high-quality trucks, as well as control of an amazing one-third of heavy-duty truck sales. The company led the industry during the last two decades of the twentieth century with improvements in cab and suspension design, expansion of manufacturing plants in California and Indiana, and a marketing deal to sell Volvos in the United States. Freightliner's own market strength, coupled with the resources of a global corporate leader, meant that its future appears quite secure.

A limited-edition Classic XL 84-inch SleeperCab led Freightliner's parade of new models in 1999. The new sleeper cab extended Freightliner's largest offering by more than one foot. The company targeted driver-friendly features, such as cabinet and storage areas, a double bunk, and a lounge option that allows a driver to convert the lower bunk to a work or dining area with its own table.

Freightliner also unveiled two new Century Class models in 1999, boosting the Century Class line to 14 configurations. The 70-inch mid-roof XT (for extra tall) SleeperCab was designed with bulk and

Pictured at the 1991 International Truck Show in Anaheim, California, this new Freightliner has fender skirts on the front—unusual for a tractor like this.

This clean-looking Freightliner features the long-hood and flat-top sleeper configuration. This rig is based in New York but runs coast-to-coast hauling machinery.

A Freightliner cab-over is seen here at a Las Vegas truck stop, its cargo an International Paystar dump truck from West Virginia. Freightliner is one of the few truck builders that are still making a cab-over model.

flatbed haulers in mind. It added 10 inches of interior headroom in a profile that was aerodynamically compatible with tankers and flatbeds.

The 34-inch SleeperCab, on the other hand, was targeted to regional haulers who occasionally spend an overnight on the road and want a bunk big enough to log legal rest time. The 34-inch SleeperCab could also be used to pull the "B" doubles common in Canada's western provinces while staying within the overall length limits. A Day Cab was also added to the Argosy family of cab-overs, bringing that product line to five models.

Freightliner also offered a choice of three new audio systems from Delphi Delco. The emphasis on customer convenience signaled an important development in truck marketing.

Meanwhile, in a bold move to change and improve service to all highway customers, Freightliner Corporation acquired an ownership interest in TravelCenters of America (TA), the only nationwide

network of full-service highway travel centers at that time. Freightliner augmented its existing network of 300 dealers with 124 TA express parts and service locations in 39 states. Freightliner was the first truck manufacturer in North America to undertake a comprehensive partnership with a nationwide service center provider. Freightliner President Jim Hebe said, "By combining the service forces of our Freightliner dealers with the top-rated TravelCenters of America service network, we are aggressively stepping up our support of customers with increased locations, service options, and service capacity and amenities that are available 24 hours a day, 7 days a week." Its centers provided maintenance and repair services to some 2,800 truck drivers a day in 1998.

Freightliner's independent dealer network remained the front line of service for Freightliner trucks, while TravelCenters of America focused on express service and minor repair work, such as brake, electrical, heating, and air conditioning, Department of Transportation

Aside from niche marketing, Sterling is gaining acceptance with long-distance truckers. While it may take a little time, the name Sterling may, once again, be as famous as it was back in the 1930s through the 1950s. Since Sterling is part of Freightliner, it has a network of support from the parent company.

The new Sterling is aiming at niche marketing and specialized areas of trucking, like this new dump truck with pup trailer designed for the construction industry.

inspections, and trailer maintenance and repair. The aggressive Freightliner marketing strategy helped explain the phenomenal growth of this line of trucks. In 1998, Freightliner earned a record 33.1 percent of the Class 8 heavy truck market. For the first time in its history, Freightliner became the top producer of Class 4–8 commercial vehicles in North America, producing 128,250 trucks. Freightliner Corporation was the leading heavy truck manufacturer in North America. As a DaimlerChrysler company today, Freightliner is part of the world's largest commercial vehicle manufacturer.

CHAPTER 4

KENWORTH

We started building that first truck to keep help around.
—Ed Hahn, mechanic (1915)

Kenworth has a reputation as a leader in diesel truck manufacturing today, and its history shows how marketing savvy has played an important role in the development of the industry.

KENWORTH ORIGINS:
AN EARLY NORTHWEST PLAYER

The Pacific Northwest experienced dramatic change at the dawn of the twentieth century. Horses and carriages were being replaced by motor-driven vehicles. Roads were being paved faster on the West Coast than any other part of the nation. The Northwest, in particular, was in need of trucks to meet the demands of the timber industry. Challenging weather and terrain spawned the need for roads and vehicles that could be used on them. At the same time, Seattle had become a key port and vital link to the nation's business markets in Asia. Seattle businessman Edgar Worthington was managing his mother's building, which happened to be occupied by a car and truck dealership. Edgar's tenant was the Gerlinger Motor Car Company, and he noticed that business was brisk. People wanted cars. The repair business was profitable but unpredictable. Brothers Louis and Edgar Gerlinger originally sold cars in Portland, Oregon, and the early models required a lot of maintenance. Gerlinger mechanic Ed Hahn

told company historians how the earliest truck manufacturing was born out of a need to keep busy in a fledgling industry:

IN THOSE DAYS THERE WERE SO FEW TRUCKS AND CARS AND THERE WAS NO UNION, SO AS A MECHANIC, YOU HAD TO STAND AROUND THE GARAGE—OR IN THIS CASE, THE REPAIR SHOP—AND WAIT FOR WORK TO COME IN. SOMETIMES YOU MADE FIVE DOLLARS A WEEK AND SOMETIMES YOU DIDN'T HARDLY MAKE YOUR BOARD; THEN YOU'D HAVE TO LEAVE AND GO DO OTHER WORK—SAWMILL WORK OR SOMETHING ELSE. SO WE STARTED BUILDING THAT FIRST TRUCK TO KEEP HELP AROUND.

That first truck was called the Gersix, a six-cylinder vehicle built in 1915 of structural steel and weighing more than two tons. The rugged truck took nearly one year to complete and was also sold as the Model G. Hahn said he and one other mechanic worked on the truck around other jobs: " . . . as soon as something came in, we'd drop it and go overhaul a man's truck or reline some brakes. As soon as we finished all that, we'd go back to working on the first truck again—sometimes nothing would come in and we'd work all day on it." The Gersix was one of the first six-cylinder trucks at a time when four-cylinder engines were the norm. The Gerlingers thought they

"Beyond Obsession" is what Roger and Heather Hogeland call their 1999 W900L Kenworth. Together, this husband and wife team run cross-country, hauling poultry and produce.

A 1938 Kenworth is seen here at an indoor truck show. This KW has been in just about every trucking magazine there is and has been featured in truck shows coast-to-coast.

Schott Trucking & Farming of Tipton, California, owns this beautiful 1946 low-mount Kenworth, which has been in the family for over 50 years. Only recently restored and to show-truck quality, this KW definitely draws attention wherever it goes.

Exley Produce Express ran the West Coast with an all-Kenworth fleet for over 30 years. The Exley KWs were red and white.

could sell more-powerful trucks to haulers struggling up steep hills on winding country roads.

It took the Gerlinger brothers nearly a year to build that first truck, and it had no cab. They built a meager two trucks in the second year of production. They struggled to prove to loggers that their Gersix could meet the challenges of the lumber business, and they also had trouble obtaining raw materials at an affordable price. Steel was in short supply. The world was heading into war.

Edgar Worthington and his partner, Captain Frederick Kent, saw an opportunity, purchased the company in 1917, and renamed it the Gersix Motor Company. By 1919, Frederick Kent retired from the business. Son Harry Kent, known as a bottom-liner in business circles, joined Worthington. As late as 1921, Gersix was still selling the Model G without a cab or body to area loggers. Now, the company was about to grow. They enclosed the cab and looked to the future. Fifty-three Gersix trucks were sold in 1922. The partners used $60,000 to reincorporate and renamed the company "Ken-Worth" after the two principal stockholders Harry Kent and Edgar Worthington. The Kenworth Motor Truck Company was born, and headquarters were established in Seattle. They built a new factory in downtown Seattle and managed to produce a whopping 78 trucks in 1923 and 80 trucks in 1924. The Model K replaced the Model G as

In 1954 Kenworth came out with the CBE (cab-beside-engine) model. While it wasn't the most attractive Kenworth, it was accepted by some fleets.

In this 1964 picture, we see Larry Ford's older KW conventional with a homemade sleeper behind the cab. This dark blue rig hauled produce from Los Angeles to Montana.

the heaviest truck in the Gersix line. Now production increased dramatically: Kenworth built 200 trucks in 1925. Trucks were needed to fulfill the demands of a booming timber and logging industry, and Kenworth was positioned to take advantage of the opportunity.

Kenworth became known as a custom truck builder. Vernon Smith, an incredible salesman, had come to Gersix in 1922. He had a record of being able to sell Diamond Ts in St. Louis, and he was determined to go west and prosper in sales management. Smith, according to Kenworth's John Cannon, sold trucks by offering customers anything they wanted:

> Vernon Smith would go out and sell some trucks with this or that specification, and then he'd come back to the plant and say, 'Here, I have the sales, now we have to build them.' So, it came not as a designed thing, but more or less as the state-of-the-market at the time.

Vernon Smith also was willing to take nearly anything in trade—horse or old truck—to sell a new truck. The company would rebuild

In this 1969 picture, a high-mount dark blue Kenworth is seen in a desert, on the way to Lake Havasu, Arizona. The truck was operated by Contractors Cargo of South Gate, California, and it was hauling pieces of the London Bridge.

The Kenworth bullnose cab-over was a popular truck in the 1950s. Here in this 1968 picture is one of Reeves Trucking's KWs from Fort Morgan, Colorado, pulling a straight-deck livestock trailer.

Lloyd Hibner of Springfield, Missouri, ran this chromed-out blue Kenworth into Los Angeles on a weekly basis. This picture was taken in 1964 at Steve's Richfield Truck Stop on Alameda Street in Los Angeles.

First making its appearance around 1955, the Model 521 was an interim model. It soon gave way to the famous K Model that came out in the late 1950s.

trade-ins and resell them. With others building standard trucks, Kenworth's custom production continued to soar. Kenworth was an early but brief manufacturer of trucks in Vancouver, Canada. Perhaps they were too far ahead of their time, because profits didn't yet support Canadian truck building. The government taxed importation of finished products, but tariffs could be avoided by shipping parts across the border and assembling the trucks there. The company built four- and six-cylinder trucks during this period.

Having increased production to more than 100 trucks a year, Harry Kent took over as president in 1929. The company built 3-ton Models 184 and 185, and 10-ton Models 345 and NT. Unaware of the impending stock market crash, Kent opened a new Seattle factory. It was an optimistic time in which companies planned for continued huge growth. Then came the Great Depression. Production faltered. Loans defaulted. Kenworth survived by moving into the fire truck market in 1932. Kenworth could build custom trucks and saw how this translated into a new market: "Every fire chief felt that he was the world's leading designer of fire trucks, and he wanted some of his ideas incorporated into the fire trucks," said Kenworth's Murray Aitken. Harry Kent died in 1937, and Phillip Johnson came from Boeing to lead the company through the war years. He died in 1944.

Rob Hilarides owns this 1957 Kenworth, seen here in 1980. Hilarides hauls milk from various dairies in the Tulare area of California.

Kenworth conventional truck and trailers with "boxes" are a rare sight, so when this late 1950s rig ran the roads in Central California, heads would turn.

In 1945 Pacific Car and Foundry acquired Kenworth. William Pigott, Sr., had founded Seattle Car Manufacturing Company in 1905 at a plant in West Seattle. Seattle Car eventually merged with Twohy Brothers of Portland to become Pacific Car and Foundry Company. Control of the company was sold in 1924 to the American Car and Foundry Company. The economic collapse in 1929 took its toll. According to company records:

PAUL PIGOTT, SON OF THE FOUNDER, ACQUIRED A MAJOR INTEREST IN THE COMPANY FROM AMERICAN CAR IN 1934. UNDER HIS LEADERSHIP, THE COMPANY EXPANDED ITS PRODUCTS AND INTRODUCED THE CARCO LINE OF POWER WINCHES FOR USE ON CRAWLER TRACTORS IN THE LOGGING INDUSTRY.

Ed C. Greenwalt leased this early 1960s Kenworth cab-over cattle truck to Triple Bee Meat Packing of Vernon, California. The mint green cab (almost white) and dark green body and trailer suggest that this KW pulled cattle at one time for Allan Arthur Livestock Transportation.

51

Gene Badders of Terra Bella, California, owns this rare 1963 Kenworth wide-hood that once belonged to Bob Bennett. This KW pulls a set of doubles, hauling hay and alfalfa.

George Cushnie drove this 1963 tilt-hood Kenworth, which was the pride of the Connolly Transportation fleet. Connolly was the contract carrier for Hamms Beer in California during the 1950s and 1960s.

As with all other truck manufacturers, World War II had a major impact. Pacific Car and Foundry's Renton plant built Sherman tanks. The firm also assisted the war effort by manufacturing dry docks and steel tugboats.

When the company acquired Kenworth, it moved Kenworth's plant to a new 24-acre site in south Seattle. A milestone of the period was development of the "bruck"–a combination 17-passenger bus with truck hauling space in the back. The innovation failed miserably. Pacific Car and Foundry continued to expand in the heavy truck market with the purchase of Peterbilt Motors Company in 1958. The company's involvement was broad. Its structural steel

1964 was one of the last years that a trucker could order the older-style Kenworth with the small classic cab, butterfly hood, all-steel fenders, and single headlights. Earl Failla decided to do just that in ordering his new KW dump truck from J. T. Jenkins, the Kenworth dealer for the Los Angeles area. 1964 was also the first year of the newly designed Kenworth conventional, and if it was placed side-by-side with today's KW conventional, one would see some striking similarities.

Guy Wilson leased this 1966 KW cab-over to Hopper Truck Lines of Phoenix, Arizona. Aside from owning this neat KW, Wilson owned a truck customizing shop in Commerce, California, and decided to put a vinyl top on this rig. How many Class 8 trucks have vinyl tops?

LOWER LEFT: Bill Lynch, dba Northwest Fruit & Produce of Wapato, Washington, owned this sanitary Kenworth. This tractor's narrow tilt-hood and 60-inch Mercury walk-in sleeper made it the talk of the interstates.

BELOW: Golden West Livestock Transportation of Utah hauled cattle and sheep with this set of Wilson livestock "boxes." This rig appears to be a 1972 K Model.

Raider Trucking of Phoenix, Arizona, owns "Alexis," a Kenworth Aerodyne cab-over. This picture was taken at a King 8 truck show in Las Vegas around 1988.

The Kenworth T600, often called "the Anteater," first came on the trucking scene in 1985 and was an instant success. Because of its aerodynamic style, the T600 boasted better fuel mileage, as the price of diesel fuel was constantly climbing. Here we see one of Lynden Transfer's T600 being cleaned.

division fabricated raw materials for the Space Needle, built for the Seattle World's Fair in 1962.

By 1960, Pacific Car and Foundry became an international truck manufacturer. Kenworth acquired an interest in Kenworth Mexicana. In 1966 Kenworth Trucks opened an assembly plant in Melbourne, Australia, to reach that market. At the same time, the company also launched its own financing arm for the efficient sales of ever more expensive trucks. The company's Dynacraft division sold Kenworth and Peterbilt parts. Pacific Car and Foundry Company updated its image in 1972 with the new name Paccar. The 1980s saw Paccar branch out into truck leasing. At the same time, this global-minded company acquired Foden Trucks in England. The corporation added DAF Trucks of the Netherlands and Leyland Trucks of England in the 1990s to its broad line. Leyland manufactures trucks in the 6–18-ton commercial segment at its plant in Lancashire.

KENWORTH OVERVIEW

Kenworth's truck designs led the industry with the first factory-installed six-cylinder gas engine. In 1933 Kenworth became the first

Hauling milk in all kinds of weather presents no problems to trucker Jim Sharkey of Twin Falls, Idaho. This KW hauls for Darigold Products, a favorite brand of dairy items in the West.

The massive and mighty T800 is seen here in the wide-open spaces north of Las Vegas, Nevada. This unit hauls oversized loads for Vosburg Equipment Company of Las Vegas. Notice the size of the radiator area.

The T2000 Kenworth is the latest model designed for long-haul truckers of the new millennium. Because of its sleek aerodynamic design, many truckers refer to the T2000 as a "Dodge Ram on steroids."

American truck manufacturer to install diesel engines as standard equipment. The company followed White, GMC, and International by experimenting in the 1930s with sleeper designs. Cab-over-engine designs, use of aluminum parts, and hydraulic brakes became important after passage of the Motor Carrier Act. The Model 516 was KW's first on-highway COE in 1936. And Kenworth is also known for refinements to the shovelnose conventional truck. KW's conventional trucks in the 1940s and 1950s featured fender-mounted headlights. The M-1 military "wreckers" helped establish the company's reputation during World War II, and the modern semi-truck began to emerge in the 1950s. The bullnose cab-over became popular as new state laws restricted lengths and weights. The K100 cab-over remained basically unchanged from the late 1950s until 1964, when the grille was updated. KW's Model 521, introduced in 1955, featured a 72-inch sleeper cab. It was the replacement for the bullnose, which was phased out a few years later. By 1958, COE's featured a limited-tilting cab.

Kenworth also experimented with a cab-beside-engine (CBE) "half cab" in 1954. As the name implies, the rig was less than half the width of a standard cab, making it extremely lightweight with excellent visibility through a single windshield.

KW produced the 853 for oil field work in the Middle East and the 802 for earth moving in America. The 900 series, introduced in 1956, became important in equipment transport to oil exploration sites in the Northern Yukon. These were heavy-duty, no-frills truck models.

Conventional models such as the 525 helped the company continue to meet a broad range of trucking needs. Engine access improved with hoods that could tilt forward as much as 90 degrees. In 1962, Kenworth introduced the Model 925 which featured the modern wide hood found on trucks today.

Engines were getting larger. By the 1950s, Kenworth used a 220-horsepower Cummins motor. Shifting gears became more complex with main and auxiliary transmissions. At the same time, larger, heavier loads meant the need for lighter trucks. In 1959, KW began building its conventional trucks with "Uniglas" all-fiberglass front ends that could be flipped over for easy engine access as an alternative to the conventional butterfly hood access panels.

KW Keeps On Truckin'

The 1960s were pivital years for Kenworth. The S-900, introduced in 1961, was a truck that secured the future of lighter-weight conventional models. In 1962 the 925 established the KW conventional look of a smaller cab, a long front end, and a large radiator. Longer hoods made room for V-12 diesel engines. The conventional trucks Kenworth built during the 1970s were durable on- and off-road rigs. The 900-series trucks featured broad bumpers, tall radiators, and an upright cab look. The W900 conventional came on the scene in 1964, but truckers could still order the older-style model that year. After 1964 the smaller windshield and cab gave way to the modern look. The W900 not only provided drivers with larger cabs but also redesigned instrument panels. By 1965, when Kenworth opened its Kansas City plant, truck production hit a record 2,037 vehicles.

In 1973, Kenworth celebrated 50 years of trucking by selling more than 10,000 vehicles, and this led to the opening of a plant in Chillicothe, Ohio, the following year. Now, the company was producing raised-roof Aerodyne sleeper models along with its ever-popular conventional trucks.

Richard Dini Walker is known to truckers as "Mr. Kenworth." And for good reason: Walker eats, sleeps, and breathes trucks, and the tattoos on his body are a walking testimony to Kenworth trucks.

Kenworth's "Ant-eater" models evolved in the 1980s with a tapered hood for improved aerodynamics, and this led to better fuel efficiency. The T600 improved aerodynamics by 40 percent, and the truck saved customers 22 percent on fuel over other conventional models. This became popular in an era of volatile fuel prices. Kenworth's W900L revived the long-hooded design in the 1990s.

By 1993, Kenworth had opened yet another plant in Renton, Washington. Trucks continued to be manufactured in Seattle, Chillicothe, Canada, and Mexico. The sleek AeroCab was introduced as an integrated cab/sleeper truck. Kenworth continued to succeed by rounding the conventional look with the T2000 in 1996.

KENMEX

The Kenworth Mexican plant manufactures a wide range of tractors and cabs, including the Aerocab and T2000. Since 1995, Paccar has been sole owner of Kenworth Mexicana. Paccar, known for Kenworth, Peterbilt, Foden, DAF, and Leyland trucks, also manufactures truck winches and parts.

Since 1966, the Peterbilt PB330 also has been manufactured in Mexico. Kenworth Mexicana has sold trucks in Chile, Russia, Colombia, Ghana, Canada, the United States, and Puerto Rico. By the end of 1998, Kenworth Mexicana employed 1,930 people—a dramatic rise from Mexico's 1995 economic crisis when only a few hundred worked at the plant.

"The truck manufacturing industry is challenged to produce vehicles with greater fuel savings, endurance and durability, lighter in weight, easier to repair and more comfortable interiors," said Paccar's David J. Hovind of the need for the T2000. "We have presented a product that, no doubt, will set new standards in the tractor truck industry, a product created with a futuristic vision, technologically advanced and designed with the carrier companies and operator's needs in mind," said Marco Antonio Dávila, Kenworth Mexicana's Sales Director.

KENWORTH'S FUTURE

Kenworth emphasized quality, durability, and driver comfort as it rode into the new century. It held 10.6 percent of Class 8 market sales in 1998, making it the fifth most popular rig. It was stronger in the

Pictured in this 1970 photo is a 1964 Kenmex. like its counterpart to the north, this Kenmex is every bit a Kenworth. Kenworth has been making trucks in Mexico for over 40 years at its factory in Mexicali, B.C. (Baja, California), supplying both Central and South America with quality trucks.

Class 8 market than in lighter-weight truck sales. Kenworth sales trends were above 11 percent of the market in 1999 as demand for new heavy trucks continued to soar. Moreover, sister truck builder Peterbilt was not far behind. Paccar, through its sales of Kenworth and Peterbilt trucks, accounted for one-fifth of all heavy truck sales. Out on the road, you are about as likely to see one of these two nameplates as the highly popular Freightliner and Navistar trucks. The Kenworth KW, therefore, appears to have its nose out front with the industry leaders. The success of Kenworth has given the Gerlinger brothers, their garage mechanics, and businessman Harry Kent a place in the history of the development of the American semi-truck.

CHAPTER 5

PETERBILT

Since 1993, Peterbilt has introduced more new products and services than at any time in its fifty-seven year history—trucks and sleepers that appeal to a broader range of industries. . .

—Peterbilt company statement (1999)

Paccar would be a successful truck manufacturer if it produced only Kenworth trucks. But the corporation is lucky enough to also have the Peterbilt line.

PETERBILT ORIGINS:
THE CALIFORNIA CONNECTION

Frank and William Fageol foresaw the motorized future in 1899 when they built a car in Iowa that ran on gasoline. A decade later, they moved their garage to Oakland, California. Fageol Motors Company was founded in 1916 with the financial help of W. H. Bill, who became president and the inspiration for the name "Bill-Bilt." Fageol Motors began by focusing on expensive farm tractors and luxury cars and then expanded into bus and truck manufacturing when World War I pushed the nation toward thinking only about necessities. The need for buses grew because California was a leader in paved roads. The conventional four-cylinder gasoline-powered trucks were popular, particularly with the logging industry. The Fageol twins, however, were doomed by a bad business deal.

In 1924, American Car & Foundry wanted to build trucks in Kent, Ohio, but the market was competitive. They turned to the Fageol brothers. Fageol, always looking for a new angle on the business, agreed to work with American Car & Foundry and jumped in headfirst into a partnership. The pool was empty. By 1929 Fageol was in bankruptcy, and by 1932 the full effects of the Great Depression forced Fageol into receivership.

The Waukesha Motor Company, which had produced engines for Fageol trucks, assumed control and kept the company in the truck business through the turbulent 1930s. But the last Fageol rolled off the assembly line at the end of 1938 after Sterling Motors Company of Milwaukee had taken over. Sterling wanted Fageol's sales distribution network but sold the manufacturing and assembly plants to T. A. Peterman, a logging entrepreneur from Tacoma, Washington, who wanted to build his own trucks under his Peterman Manufacturing Company. He liked the "Bill-Bilt" Fageols, and decided to produce trucks under the "Peterbilt" nameplate. The first Peterbilt trucks used the Fageol egg-crate-style grille, but as production inched up during World War II, Peterbilt trucks took on their modern, sleek look. The trucks continued to be manufactured at Fageol's Oakland plant. According to company records:

WHILE HENRY FORD WAS CRANKING OUT HUNDREDS OF TRUCKS A DAY, T. A. PETERMAN WAS SETTING HIS SIGHTS ON BUILDING A HUNDRED

Pat Higgins drove this neat 1995 Model 379 Peterbilt for Stewart Construction Company of Las Vegas, Nevada. At night you can see purple neon lights under this rig.

"Brutus" is a 1987 Peterbilt Model 379 owned by Gary Word of Kansas. This tractor sports a 350-inch wheelbase with an extended back of the cab. Try driving this one through downtown Boston. The sleeper on "Brutus" is a combination of two Kenworth Aerodyne sleepers. This rig runs cross-country, carrying automotive parts.

Pictured at a 1989 truck show is this 1939 Peterbilt, one of the first Peterbilt trucks made, after the name was changed from Fageol Trucks.

This 1947 low-mount Peterbilt bobtail performs road service calls for truckers in the Reno-Sparks area of Nevada.

TRUCKS A YEAR, CONCENTRATING ON QUALITY, NOT QUANTITY. FACTORY RECORDS STATE THAT FOURTEEN TRUCKS WERE ACTUALLY SHIPPED THAT PARTIAL FIRST YEAR, AND THE 1940 PRODUCTION TOTAL FOR A WHOLE YEAR WAS EIGHTY-TWO UNITS. THE INCREDIBLE SPEED WITH WHICH THE PETERBILT TRUCK GAINED ACCEPTANCE IN THE TRUCKING INDUSTRY WAS A TRIBUTE TO PRODUCT QUALITY. ONE MAJOR REASON FOR THIS WAS THAT PETERMAN SENT ENGINEERS OUT INTO THE FIELD TO FIND OUT FIRSTHAND WHAT TRUCKERS NEEDED AND WANTED. PETERBILT ENGINEERS DID NOT GO TO THE DRAWING BOARD UNTIL THEY'D GOTTEN THEIR BOOTS DIRTY FINDING OUT EXACTLY WHAT WAS REQUIRED OF THEIR DESIGN. SHORTLY AFTER THE OUTBREAK OF WORLD WAR II, PETERBILT WENT INTO PRODUCTION OF HEAVY-DUTY TRUCKS TO FULFILL GOVERNMENT CONTRACTS. THE ENGINEERING AND PRODUCTION EXPERTISE GAINED FROM THE DESIGN AND PRODUCTION OF THESE TRUCKS ENABLED PETERBILT TO RETURN TO COMMERCIAL PRODUCTION AFTER THE WAR.

PETERBILT OVERVIEW

The script chrome Peterbilt nameplate, said to be T. A. Peterman's signature, is a symbol of style and class. From 1941 to 1944 production was limited. When Peterman died in 1945, his company had produced

A low-mount 1940s Peterbilt is seen in this 1966 picture pulling for Valley Motor Lines. Valley later merged with Consolidated Copperstate Lines to form Valley/Copperstate Lines, and ran LTL and TL freight from California to Texas and back.

A 1948 high-mount Peterbilt is seen here unloading steel for Gary Steel Company of Los Angeles. This rig was once a lumber hauler for Dan Boone Trucking. Under the hood a 290-horsepower Cummins engine can be found, backed by a five-speed main and three-speed auxiliary transmission.

just 225 trucks. Investors bought the company in 1947 and renamed it Peterbilt Motors. Production jumped to 350. Sometime between 1949 and 1951 the now traditional Peterbilt signature was standardized on the red oval background found on nameplates today.

The new Peterbilt took advantage of lightweight aluminum parts. While the traditional Waukeshau gasoline engines remained available, it was now possible to order a Cummins diesel. Peterbilt began as a conventional truck, but cab-overs followed. The Model 350 appeared in 1952 with a snubnose front. The Model 351 was a conventional introduced in 1954.

In 1956, Peterbilt unveiled the "Dromedary" or drom box—a short cargo trailer set on an extended wheelbase behind the cab. The fifth wheel sat behind the van. This allowed an unhooked tractor to carry small loads, increasing the flexibility of the truck.

But the Model 352 cab-over introduced that same year was more popular. The truck could be ordered with a either a standard behind-the-driver sleeper or an above-the-driver penthouse sleeper already common on White Freightliner trucks.

This 1966 photo shows a 1951 Peterbilt truck and trailer, owned by Signal Oil Company of Montebello, California. The first two numbers on the bumper always signified the year of the truck for the Signal fleet.

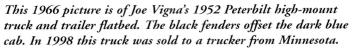
This 1966 picture is of Joe Vigna's 1952 Peterbilt high-mount truck and trailer flatbed. The black fenders offset the dark blue cab. In 1998 this truck was sold to a trucker from Minnesota.

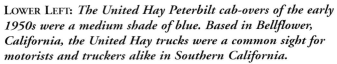
LOWER LEFT: The United Hay Peterbilt cab-overs of the early 1950s were a medium shade of blue. Based in Bellflower, California, the United Hay trucks were a common sight for motorists and truckers alike in Southern California.

BELOW: Anderson Dairy of Las Vegas, Nevada, ran this old Peterbilt cab-over with a drom box behind the cab. In this 1956 photo, the rig was at the L.A. Union Stockyards unloading some dairy cattle. The drom box was used for carrying milk products.

Ed White leased this clean dark green 1953 Peterbilt cab-over to Paxton Truck Company of Montebello, California. Paxton was a leading carrier of steel for the state of California from the 1940s until the early 1970s.

Shown in Indio, California, in the summer of 1965, this 1957 Peterbilt cab-over has a drom box that was used to haul cattle for Hilton's Cow-Tel of Imperial, California.

Today's Peterbilt trucks have been influenced by the 1958 sale of the company to Pacific Car and Foundry, the owners of Kenworth:

AFTER PETERMAN'S DEATH, COMPANY OWNERSHIP PASSED TO HIS WIDOW, IDA. SHE SOLD THE ASSETS, BUT NOT THE UNDERLYING LAND, TO A GROUP OF SEVEN PETERBILT MANAGEMENT EMPLOYEES WITH THE PURPOSE OF PRESERVING AND EXPANDING THE COMPANY. BUT IN 1958, MRS. PETERMAN ANNOUNCED HER PLANS TO DEVELOP THE PLANT SITE INTO A SHOPPING CENTER, AND PETERBILT'S OWNERS WERE FACED WITH THE DILEMMA OF RAISING TWO MILLION DOLLARS FOR A NEW PLANT. SINCE THE OWNERS, HEADED BY PRESIDENT LLOYD LUNDSTROM, WERE APPROACHING RETIREMENT AGE AND DID NOT WANT TO INCUR A LARGE LONG-TERM DEBT, THEY PUT THE COMPANY UP FOR SALE. PAUL PIGOTT OF PACIFIC CAR AND FOUNDRY SHOWED AN IMMEDIATE INTEREST AND, ON JUNE 24, 1958, ACQUIRED PETERBILT MOTORS AS A WHOLLY OWNED SUBSIDIARY. ONE YEAR LATER, PACIFIC CAR STARTED CONSTRUCTION OF A MODERN 176,000–SQUARE-FOOT MANUFACTURING FACILITY IN NEWARK, CALIFORNIA.

Production ended in Oakland and was shifted to Newark. Paccar knew marketing and mass production. About 21,000 Peterbilts rolled off assembly lines during the 1960s. The success led to the opening

This dark blue 1954 Peterbilt is owned by Glenn Simonian. This truck and trailer hauls Simonian-made products to his various clients.

Anyone old enough to remember the clean fleet of dark blue LT Macks and Peterbilts hauling for Dr. Ross Dog Food is probably collecting Social Security benefits today. These super-clean trucks were ahead of their time.

In this 1966 picture, Marlo Diaz drives a new Peterbilt for McKesson & Robbins Chemical Company of Commerce, California. This truck had just been delivered by Motor Truck Distributors, the Los Angeles Peterbilt dealer at that time.

This sharp dark blue and white 1964 Peterbilt was the pride of the Montana Brands Produce fleet of Diamond Ts and Peterbilts. This picture made the cover of a truckers magazine in 1965 and was taken at Steve's Richfield Truck Stop in Los Angeles.

of a new plant in Madison, Tennessee, in 1970—a facility that cranked out 72,000 trucks in that decade alone. Peterbilt offered a 110-inch cab-over, again following the White Freightliner lead.

By 1980, Peterbilt's third assembly plant opened in Denton, Texas. Peterbilt phased out the Model 352 cab-over in favor of the redesigned 362, which offered the option of a one-piece flat windshield common today. The Model 362 continues as a very popular cab-over truck. Production ended in Newark by the late 1980s, but continued in Madison and Denton. The sleeker Model 372 was introduced in 1988 under the nickname "Winnebago."

GLOBAL TRUCKING

Peterbilt's Model 379 today leads the manufacturer's conventional line of trucks. There is a wide range of engines up to 550 horsepower. The Peterbilt Model 385 offers a Caterpillar C-10, 350-horsepower engine. The 377A/E provides room, ride, and what the company calls "luxury." It can be equipped with Unibilt sleeper, UltraCab, or

This new 1968 Peterbilt is seen at Motor Truck Distributors, the company that sold this model, along with several others, to the Los Angeles Department of Water & Power. These off-highway models were based near Lone Pine, California. Its current owner is Cliff Wilkins of Blackwell, Oklahoma, and the truck is now a wrecker.

Unibilt Day Cab. It is available in a set-forward or a set-back front axle configuration. Driver accommodations can be tailored to the length of the haul with up to 70-inch sleepers. The 362E features a swept-back front bumper. The patented rear cab mount system adds an extra dimension of comfort and stability, while reducing cab structure stress. The 320 can be equipped with a variety of cab configurations. The 330 uses an innovative corrosion-resistant cab built from lightweight, high-strength aluminum. It has a unique two-piece flat windshield. A fuel-efficient Caterpillar 3126 engine with 210 horsepower is standard. Also available are other Caterpillar and Cummins engines up to 300 horsepower.

PETERBILT'S FUTURE

Everyone seems to agree that this Paccar company has a bright future as stiff competitor to sister company Kenworth. Peterbilt always has been and continues to stand for a classy brand of quality truck production. For the Fageol twins and T. A. Peterman, the Peterbilt logo rides high as a lasting imprint on the history of the American semi-truck.

Johnny Gregg of Calimesa, California, owned these two wide-hood transfer dumps in the early 1970s. These trucks, along with a narrow hood, were always kept in spotless condition.

In the late 1960s, in order to compete with White-Freightliner, Peterbilt introduced a 110-inch sleeper cab-over model, and success soon followed. Many of these rigs are still on the road.

Lerner Oil Company had a string of low-priced gas stations in and around Los Angeles in the 1960s and 1970s. To deliver gas to their many stations, Lerner ran this 1970 Model 359 long-hood truck and trailer.

UPPER RIGHT: *M & F Packing Company of Santa Barbara, California, had a fleet of Peterbilt 352s that ran cross-country for this now defunct chain of Sambos restaraunts.*

In this 1971 picture, a Model 352 is being weighed on a public scale on Bandini Blvd. in Vernon, California. Roscoe Wagner of Twin Falls, Idaho, hauled livestock with this truck and trailer with Wilson "boxes."

UPPER LEFT: *Golden Bear Marketing of Glendora, California, has one of the cleanest fleets of tankers in California. Seen here is an early 1980s Peterbilt pulling a 35-foot tanker.*

ABOVE: *Seen here on an early and cold November morning near Coaldale, Nevada, is a "Pete" cab-over Model 362, hauling over 12,000 gallons of gasoline.*

This new 1990 Model 320 has a Stagg refuse body on its chassis. The Model 320 is perfect for refuse and recycling, as its low-entry cab allows the operator to get in and out easily.

The Model 372, often referred to as "The Winnebago," first came out around 1988 but never really caught on with most truckers, and production was discontinued a few years later.

This Model 362 has a drom box on the cab-over. More household goods can be carried on this tractor-trailer when a drom unit is added. This photo was taken in 1998 at the former King 8 Truck Plaza in Las Vegas, Nevada.

Bigger doesn't mean better. Take the case of In-N-Out Burgers. Their hamburgers are better, their drive-throughs are cleaner, and their big rigs are sharper than a lot of rigs that we see running the highways of today.

Right out of a Japanese monster movie, this dinosaur is about to take a bite out of Joe Burchardi's load of hay, seen here at The Wheel Inn at Cabazon, California. This Peterbilt is based in Santa Ynez, California.

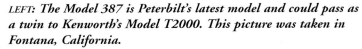

LEFT: The Model 387 is Peterbilt's latest model and could pass as a twin to Kenworth's Model T2000. This picture was taken in Fontana, California.

ABOVE, RIGHT: A late-model Peterbilt with a one-piece windshield is seen here near the California-Nevada border in 1999. Sathers Trucking of Round Lake, Minnesota, runs this rig cross-country.

Shown near Casa Grande, Arizona, in 1998, this high-roof Peterbilt is pulling for Metal Transportation Systems of New Jersey. A load of onions are seen here as a backhaul. When trucks "deadhead" or return empty, profits take a dip, as an empty truck generates no revenue.

69

CHAPTER 6

INTERNATIONAL NAVISTAR

We have exceptional products, strong customer loyalty and the best distribution channel in the industry.

—Steve Keate, Navistar Truck Division president (1999)

The family that founded International Harvester was fond of saying, "There can be no such thing as a good cheap tractor." Quality helped move the company into truck manufacturing in a big way. Navistar International Transportation Company today boasts more than 17,000 employees. It all started with a dream of modernizing American agriculture.

INTERNATIONAL ORIGINS: INNOVATION ON THE FARM

Born into invention, Cyrus McCormick saw his father try and fail to build a mechanical grain reaper during the first quarter of the nineteenth century. Dreams and persistence paid dividends when the younger McCormick obtained a patent in 1834. Still, there was no money to be made, and it was not until the 1840s that refine-ments led to sales. Around the McCormick farm in Virginia word spread of how a tractor could make farm life better. McCormick had sold more than 100 machines in 1846 when he moved production to Chicago. It was the right move at the right time. The Gold Rush in the West was about to turn the Midwest into the now sprawling nation's breadbasket, and tractors were in demand.

Although McCormick was rapidly becoming a major figure in Chicago, there were setbacks. The Great Chicago Fire of 1871 came when the inventor was already in his sixties. His decision to rebuild helped Chicago get back on its feet. Economic downturns were especially difficult as the young nation industrialized. He died at age 75 in 1884, too early to see how the farm tractor would become a harbinger of the move from horse-drawn carriages to motor vehicles.

Two Internationals at a new housing site in San Clemente, California, deliver "Tons of Quality" for Sepulveda Building Materials. The unit on the left is a 1999 model, while the tractor on the right is a 2000.

This 1940s K Model was still in active service, pulling semi-trailers as late as 1967 for *Certified Freight Lines of California.*

The West Coaster International came out shortly after the end of World War II and was also available as a cab-over. Jim Dobbas of Auburn, California, owned this truck when the photo was taken in 1995.

McCormick's son Cyrus II was just 25 when he took the reins of the McCormick Harvesting Machine Company. He had served as a secretary for his father, but he apparently could not have taken over successfully without the active involvement of his mother, Nancy, who had helped make company decisions since her marriage in 1857.

The beginning of the twentieth century was a turbulent time as organized labor emerged as a force in manufacturing. A competitive tractor market helped McCormick by creating the need for an extensive sales force. With a sales force in place, product demand would rise. In 1902 the McCormicks joined competitor William Deering and others, and with the help of the $120 million backing of J. P. Morgan, they formed the International Harvester Company. The now global manufacturer was interested in work on motor cars. Within a year, designer Edward A. Johnston had come up with the Auto Buggy. After five years of producing and selling small numbers of cars, International built a production plant in Akron, Ohio, and readied for the future. The IH name meant something to a nation where agriculture was king.

Harry Bruner leased this Cherrypicker, circa 1954, to Republic Van Lines of Los Angeles. The two-tone brown Republic rigs were a common sight as they criss-crossed the United States.

This Cherrypicker, seen here with no sleeper, was owned by Desert Express, an LTL carrier that ran in California in the 1950s and 1960s. Colors for the fleet were brown and white.

This integral sleeper International was gasoline-powered and was the truck of choice for van lines in the 1950s. This picture was taken in Tucson, Arizona, in 1967.

International used the basic design of the Auto Buggy car, attached a small bed to the rear, and produced its first truck in 1909. They called it the Auto Wagon Express, and it was designed to help farmers get produce to market. The first trucks had both air- and water-cooled engines. They carried an IHC nameplate—replaced with "International" in 1914. International moved from two-cylinder to four-cylinder engines. Trucks ranged from 1/2 to 3 1/2 ton in 1915 when the company introduced new models, not only adding power, but also improving truck transmission design. IH was ready for World War I.

A conventional-looking International truck, with its long nose, emerged in the 1920s. International trucks continued to evolve. The six-cylinder engine and enclosed cabs helped create a modern look. Diesel engines came in the 1930s to add more power. The D series appeared in the late 1930s, followed by the K series truck. International produced about 100,000 World War II military vehicles. The square look of the International truck was redesigned in 1934. Drivers nicknamed this truck with its agricultural roots the "Cornbinder."

This 1950s International dump truck was spotted in Massachusetts in 1988. It features a set-back front axle and also has diamond-plate fenders. Bold striping is popular on trucks in New England.

An International Emeryville cab-over with integral sleeper is seen here at a Wyoming truck stop in 1965. Notice the addition of a homemade sheep deck atop this semi-trailer.

"Just Coastin" is what this International says on the side of its radiator. This long-hood conventional was a favorite of truckers on the West Coast from the 1950s into the early 1960s.

Another Emeryville seen in Tucson in 1967. The Emeryville was an instant hit with truckers on both coasts of the United States and especially among the many truckers who leased their equipment to the van lines.

By the end of the war International was established as a major truck manufacturer. In response to postwar demand, the company opened its famous Emeryville, California, plant as it redesigned its K series truck. Cummins diesel engines were becoming very popular. The K series truck, produced both in Emeryville and Fort Wayne, Indiana, helped International capture a significant chunk of the Class 8 market. In 1946, IH unveiled the "West Coaster"—a large-cab conventional truck with room for a driver and two passengers. The W model offered International customers a cab-over-engine design.

Production of the KB, the largest of the K series trucks, ended in 1949. The 1950s brought the Comfo-Vision cab and one-piece windshield design. International's "Cherrypicker" cab-over had a rounded look.

IH introduced the L and R series trucks in the mid-1950s. By the late 1950s, a conventional IH might be powered with a

The International conventional seen here was often referred to as "The Donald Duck" International. A common sight in the 1960s, this model truck and trailer is hauling petroleum for Richfield (now known as Arco Oil Co.).

As a day-cab (nonsleeper), the Emeryville enjoyed much popularity. The Emeryville seen here is a 1965 model, the last year it was made. Powerine Oil Company of Santa Fe Springs, California, used this truck and trailer to deliver gasoline and diesel fuel to its many service stations.

200-horsepower Cummins engine. The Emeryville cab-over of this period became known as the "Highbinder." It featured recessed headlights, a split two-piece windshield, and a flat, square grille. The cab had some rounding to soften its overall appearance. The truck was available in sleeper and nonsleeper models until 1965.

The Emeryville was replaced with the CO-4000 cab-over, which was built until 1967. The VCO offered a V-8 gasoline engine, while the DCO was the diesel version. In 1974 the Transtar name appeared in the CO series truck, and this continued until 1981.

The IH conventional 4300 series truck originated in the early 1970s and was the company's most popular heavy-duty model. Despite its popularity, however, the company was in trouble.

INTERNATIONAL OVERVIEW

During 1979 and 1980, International truck production was severely damaged by what some have termed a "crippling" strike. The nation's agriculture industry was in crisis by the early 1980s, and International—a company born of farm success—now faltered. At the same time, the fuel shortages of the 1970s had led to government mandates for lighter and more fuel-friendly trucks. International was

The CO4000 replaced the Emeryville in late 1965. Like the Emeryville before it, the CO4000 did well in sales.

A Model 2574 is seen here in downtown Boston in 1988. Many of these models are still in use today, mostly for making local deliveries.

The 8300 series International is still a popular truck today. This one was seen in Missouri, but you can see the 8300 Model in any part of the United States.

unprepared to deal with change. The company had lost its bearings in the half century since a visionary mother and son had led this giant through earlier troubles.

In 1986 International sold the farm equipment division to Case-Tenneco along with the International Harvester name and logo. The truck division name was changed to Navistar. Now focused on big-rig truck sales, Navistar re-emerged with a resolve to conquer the competitive market.

NAVISTAR'S CORPORATE APPROACH

Today the Navistar International Corporation is headquartered in Chicago's NBC Tower, and the more than 17,000 employees are at 40 locations around the globe. This Fortune 500 giant builds trucks, school buses, engines, and parts. Navistar stock, traded on the New York Stock Exchange, has been very profitable for investors during

Based in Oakland, California, this Model 9670 gets lots of attention as it delivers groceries to the many Safeway stores in Northern California.

This Model 9800 with a set-back front axle is pulling a set of bottom dumps at Lone Mountain, not far from Las Vegas, Nevada. This model built until March 1999, when production ceased in the United States. Many are still in use and can be seen pulling containers in most of the larger cities.

the 1990s. "The improvement in our gross margins clearly shows that we continue to be successful with our strategies for greater efficiency," says chairman, president, and chief executive officer John R. Horne.

For nearly two decades, International has led the United States and Canada in combined medium and heavy truck sales, and it leads the world in 160 to 300 horsepower midrange diesel engine sales. Navistar heavy truck sales are part of a larger corporate reach that includes medium trucks, school buses, engines, parts, and financial services. The International brand carries a lot of weight in such places as Brazil, Mexico, South Africa, the Middle East, and Australia.

Navistar's 9400I is typical of a truck ready for the global marketplace. It is designed with a sculpted hood, a curved wraparound windshield, a stylized chassis, and aerodynamics for efficiency. A Pro Sleeper in the all-aluminum cab is offered with 51-inch Lo-Roof and Hi-Rise options, and the 72-inch Hi-Rise and Sky-Rise alternatives.

NAVISTAR'S EAGLE AND THE NEXT GENERATION

Navistar headed into the new century with the International Eagle 9900, a Class 8 premium conventional tractor model. The new Eagle featured a long-nose design, a smooth ride, a wider chrome grille, expansive hood, and headlights set in chrome. Its distinctive

Pictured here in Everett, Washington, is a Model 9300 International. The third axle, behind the cab, is activated when heavy loads are dumped into the body of the truck. Extra axles distribute weight more evenly on the highways, thus reducing damage to the roadways.

This 9200 series International is pulling a polished petroleum trailer made by Weld-It Manufacturing Company of Commerce, California. Weld-It has been in the business of making quality tank bodies and trailers for over 50 years, and their clients include some of the largest oil companies.

The Department of Water and Power for the city of Los Angeles has this 1998 International Paystar 6x6 based near Mt. Whitney, California, in the Sierra Mountains. Paystars are designed for working in rugged areas and are made in the Texas factory that once made Marmon Trucks.

This 9200 series International not only carries wood trusses but can load and unload itself, thanks to the truck-mounted crane located behind its cab. This picture was taken in Washington in 1998.

A 9400 series International is pulling two large bottom-dump trailers for Savage Industries of Utah.

appearance was augmented by external air cleaners, dual cab-mounted exhaust, and a full-width bright-finish bumper. The Eagle's 120-inch bumper-to-back-of-the-cab (BBC) dimension was designed with a set-forward front axle and 6x4 configuration. This distinctive truck is also the first model from International to offer 600-horsepower engines from Cummins and Caterpillar. Rockwell, Dana, and Eaton drivetrain components are offered as 9900 options.

It is clear that Navistar plans to continue to be a top nameplate in the field. International is positioned to seize the opportunities of the marketplace.

National Foods, located near Everett, Washington, hauls poultry feed with this 1998 9200 Model International.

The "secret" can finally be told: International trucks helped build the pyramids . . . at least the one in Las Vegas, Nevada. Las Vegas is a boomtown that never sleeps, and construction is ongoing. International trucks play an important role in the building of this city.

LEFT: *This clean Model 9670 hauls propane for the local Chevron distributor in Sparks, Nevada. A clean truck promotes a positive corporate image.*

Mt. Vernon, Washington, is home for this 9300 International and pup trailer. International has a reputation for durability in the construction industry.

This 1998 Paystar International 5000 is operating for California Metal X of Los Angeles. As a roll-off application, the International enjoys much success in the recycling industry.

About the only time that you will see a dirty Beneto Tank Lines truck is when it is raining or snowing, and even then, its trucks are cleaner than most. Seen here is a 9200 Model International truck and trailer, based in West Sacramento, California.

CHAPTER 7

FORD

Henry Ford and the Ford Motor Company are as much a part of American history as the founding of America itself.

—Stan Holtzman, author and photographer (1995)

Ford Motor Company's focus on the automobile helped make it an industry leader, but it also has led to its ultimate retreat from the big-rig market. The story begins with a man and his better idea.

FORD ORIGINS: OH HENRY!

Henry Ford had a humble beginning. Born in 1863 in Greenfield, Michigan, young Henry liked to tinker with machines at the family farm outside Dearborn. Henry's grandfather John Ford had come from Ireland and settled on 80 acres. Henry's father William Ford worked the family farm. Instead of joining the Fords in their passion for farming, Henry saw it as a problem to be solved. Horses were too slow, and Henry thought the hours spent plowing the fields were a waste. His father did not understand Henry's lack of interest in the family farm: "My father was not entirely in sympathy with my bent toward mechanics."

By the time Ford was sixteen, he was a machinist apprentice at the Drydock Engine Works. He liked fine work and at first repaired watches. "I figured out that watches were not universal necessities, and therefore people generally would not buy them," he wrote in his 1922 memoir. In 1879 he saw a Nichols-Shepard farm machine, and,

as he also reported in his memoir, he later worked repairing Westinghouse road engines:

THEY WERE SOMETIMES USED AS TRACTORS TO PULL HEAVY LOADS AND, IF THE OWNER ALSO HAPPENED TO BE IN THE THRESHING-MACHINE BUSINESS, HE HITCHED HIS THRESHING MACHINE AND OTHER PARAPHERNALIA TO THE ENGINE IN MOVING FROM FARM TO FARM. WHAT BOTHERED ME WAS THE WEIGHT AND COST. THEY WEIGHED A COUPLE OF TONS AND WERE FAR TOO EXPENSIVE TO BE OWNED BY OTHER THAN A FARMER WITH A GREAT DEAL OF LAND.

In 1885, Ford repaired an Otto four-cycle engine at the Eagle Iron Works in Detroit. He began tinkering with alternatives to steam power. He kept a shop on the farm but joined the Detroit Electric Company as engineer and machinist for $45 per month. By the 1890s, there was a lot of interest in Europe and America in putting motors on wheels. Ford initially set out to build farm tractors because of "the excessively hard labor of plowing." He said the horseless carriage was a common idea by this point, ever since the invention of the steam engine. Still, it did not yet seem practical. "Our roads were poor and we had not had the habit of getting

Bright colors bring your attention to this Ford AeroMax rig. Pulling for Baskin & Robbins Ice Cream Company, this tractor-trailer runs the Southwest, delivering America's favorite dessert.

83

This 1960s H Model Ford cab-over is in Ohio for this 1965 picture. Truckers often called this model "The Two-Story Falcon."

Though technically not a Class 8 big rig, this Ford cab-over was made from 1956 well into the 1990s, which proves the statement, "If you have a good thing, why change it?"

Working a construction site near Laughlin, Nevada, a Ford proves that it can meet the tough challenges presented by construction.

around." But he soon realized that "the horseless carriage made a greater appeal to the imagination."

In 1892 Ford finished his first motor car, which he called his "gasoline buggy," but he needed another year of refinement. It was the only automobile in Detroit and, according to Ford, "It was considered to be something of a nuisance, for it made a racket and it scared horses." He said it drew a crowd and tended to cause traffic jams of onlookers. By special permit of the mayor, Henry Ford ran the car some 1,000 miles during 1895–1896 before selling it for $200 to businessman Charles Ainsley. For a time, he joined Edison Company as general superintendent, but he quit his job on August 15, 1899, to return to his passion—the automobile. Henry designed his first truck that same year, six years after completing work on his experimental car.

The automobile was still seen as a novelty with no commercial potential. So, Ford's investors in the Detroit Auto Company sought to sell each car for "the largest possible price." This venture was later renamed Cadillac. Ford left in 1903 to form his own company based on his philosophy of building high-quality yet inexpensive vehicles.

In 1903, Ford founded the Ford Motor Company at a one-room brick shop at 81 Park Place to develop a four-cylinder motor. Ford's shop managed to build a car that defeated the now famous Winton

This L8000 AeroMax is at a local truck show. Superior Fast Freight had an entire fleet of Ford models.

from Cleveland at a race in Detroit. The "999" or "Arrow," built by Ford and designer Tom Cooper, was 80 horsepower and designed for speed. They trained a fearless professional bicycle rider named Barney Oldfield to drive the dark-horse car: "Well, this chariot may kill me," he told Ford, "but they will say afterward that I was going like hell when she took me over the bank." The "999" finished a half mile ahead of the next-closest car, and Ford had obtained valuable publicity. With the help of the Dodge brothers, Ford had built a respected motor car company. Ford disdained the fact that many in this new business lacked scruples. "Even as late as 1910 and 1911 the owner of an automobile was regarded as essentially a rich man whose money ought to be taken away from him." The early profits were found in repair and maintenance.

Earlier, in 1901, John and Horace Dodge's design and construction skills won them a contract with Oldsmobile. Not to be outdone, Henry Ford offered the Dodge boys a one-tenth share in his new company in exchange for their expertise in building motors and transmissions. The partnership held from 1902 to 1914, when Dodge Brothers incorporated. Through the 12-year period Ford trucks were built with virtually all Dodge parts.

An LTL-9000 is "getting with it" in this picture. John's Trucking of Las Vegas, Nevada, operates this truck, along with other makes.

This Ford 9000 cab-over comes from Hartford, Connecticut. Ford made the cab-over until the early 1990s.

FORD OVERVIEW

The early Model E, Ford's first truck, was a simple delivery van adapted from the basic Ford chassis. Around the country, truck designers began using the famous Model T "Tin Lizzy" chassis to build trucks. For $700, you could now be the proud owner of a wagon. Ford followed with the Model TT in 1917. The one-ton Model TT was larger and stronger than Ford's car, and more than a million

An LTA-9000 Ford is seen at a 1990 truck show in Anaheim, California.

This LTL-9000 near Everett, Washington, is set up as a truck and pup. Though Ford is no longer making Class 8 trucks (now known as Sterling), many of the Class 8 Fords are still in use.

Early sunrise catches this LTL-9000 AeroMax at a Missouri truck stop in 1994. Though there are no new AeroMax Fords being made today, they remain a common sight on the highways.

were delivered in just a decade. Henry Ford's philosophy was simple: "For most purposes, a man with a machine is a better than a man without a machine."

Ford followed the strong Model TT with Model A trucks, designed for in-town "local" delivery, and buses beginning in 1927. The Great Depression did not seem to slow the efficient-minded Ford.

The company began using dual-rear wheels and developed the flat-head V-8 engine. Before the decade ended, Ford had introduced 1-ton 350 and 1/2-ton 250 series trucks. Henry Ford's son, Edsel, succeeded him as president, but died in 1943. Henry Ford resumed the presidency for four more years until his death in 1947. Henry Ford II, Edsel's eldest son, was released from the Navy to return to the family business when his father died. After Henry's death in 1947, Henry Ford II brought the company back from the verge of bankruptcy.

Ford emerged from World War II convinced that redesigned larger trucks were the wave of the future. The F series trucks were introduced in 1948. The F-8 was a three-ton truck powered by a V-8 145-horsepower Lincoln engine. It, along with a 155-horsepower V-8, was introduced in 1952. Through the 1950s, Ford's gasoline engines grew to 277 horsepower but the company introduced its first diesel in 1959.

Ford opened a truck plant in Louisville, Kentucky, in 1969. The Louisville plant was a major investment and helped Ford sell more tractors. This era can be thought of as Ford's midlife in the heavy truck business.

Ford's NTD conventional truck and the H Model "Two Story Falcon" helped the company make inroads in the heavy truck market during the 1960s. The H Model was replaced with the W Model cab-over-engine in 1966. It featured squared edges, a two-piece flat

Here we see a 9000 series Ford cab-over in a day-cab application. Many day-cab Ford cab-overs are used for making local deliveries that don't require sleepers.

The last of the great Ford AeroMaxes is seen here at a Las Vegas truck show in 1996. The successor to this truck is now the Sterling, which is often mistaken for a Ford.

windshield, recessed headlights, a flat bumper, and large "F O R D" lettering just below the wipers.

By 1974, Ford was no longer America's best-selling truck and was trailing International and Mack. But the Detroit diesel-powered conventional Ls were just part of the truck line.

The rather ugly W was replaced by the CL Model in 1978. The CL offered handsome rounding, a two-piece grille, and a wider bumper. Eventually, Ford switched from large lettering to its scripted nameplate on the blue oval background. Production of the CL 9000 ended in 1991, despite the innovative nature of the COE. Its aluminum cab was lightweight, and its 600-horsepower engine in this configuration managed to reduce fuel and maintenance costs.

Ford's L Series trucks offered a conventional alternative. The LTL was a sturdy-looking truck. The LTL-9000, with its 36-inch sleeper adorned with dual sun-glass windows and its dual chrome exhaust stacks rising up and tailing off from behind the doors, was a popular rig for a variety of haulers.

Ford was moving into its declining years in the heavy truck market as it placed its fortunes in lighter trucks, including trucks used for in-town hauling and the blossoming consumer pickup truck market. Ford's F150, F250, and F350 lines of light trucks offered customers many alternatives, and these are the only trucks today still built by Ford.

AEROMAX

Ford's last heavy truck, the AeroMax, came in 1988. The AeroMax built upon the company success with cars and Aerostar minivans during the 1980s by capturing the public's imagination through design reinvention. The AeroMax rig, even during the late 1980s, was designed with angled corners and bumpers, flush headlights, and a tapered nose. The aerodynamic design continued to evolve during the 1990s. By 1998, Ford AeroMax production had ended, and Freightliner acquired and sold the remaining 12,645 trucks in inventory. It was truly the end of an era. Ford, like its competitors GMC and Dodge, however, continued to be popular in the lighter truck market. Henry Ford, as well as the company that carries his name, had a simple faith in the power of machinery and industry: "I think that unless we know more about machines and their use, unless we better understand the mechanical portion of life, we cannot have time to enjoy the trees, and the birds, and the flowers, and the green fields." He wrote in his 1922 book, *My Life and Work,* that trucking was at the core of modern society. "The foundations of society are the men and means to grow things, to make things, and to carry things." Ford saw the truck as an extension of the automobile, and the company's first advertisement could still be used today: "Our purpose is to construct and market an automobile specially designed for everyday wear and tear—business, professional, and family use."

CHAPTER 8

GMC

There is renewed energy at General Motors.
—John F. Smith, Jr., GMC chairman (1999)

General Motors has always been a global company. Just a year after its founding in 1908, GM purchased Bedford Motors in the United Kingdom. Today GM has operations in 73 countries and sales of cars and trucks in more than 200 countries, making it the largest U.S. exporter. General Motors employs nearly 400,000 people and has agreements with more than 30,000 supplier companies. While globalization is not new, GMC's chairman John Smith says that recently there have been many changes: "What is new is the way it is accelerating—the number of companies as well as the number of countries where they operate—and the way governments are dealing with the trend." It is difficult to imagine how GMC blossomed from humble beginnings in a Detroit garage.

GMC ORIGINS:
MOTOWN COMES ALIVE

Like many handy fellows at the dawn of the twentieth century, young Max and Morris Grabowsky were using their Detroit machine shop to fiddle with motor cars. With the backing of Barney Finn and Albert Marx, who operated a popular saloon, the Grabowskys launched what would eventually become the huge General Motors Corporation. Some time between 1900 and 1902 they sold their first one-cylinder (horizontally mounted)-engine truck. Originally named Rapid Motor Vehicle Company, the company was the first, in 1901, to manufacture cars in quantity. It was chartered in 1908, the year the first electric headlamp was introduced on its motor cars. Then, in 1909 William C. Durant bought the operation and renamed it GMC. Durant is considered the founder of the corporation.

Durant's GMC offered closed bodies as standard equipment in 1910, an electric self-starter in 1911, and all-steel-body construction in 1912. Under new leadership, GMC built its first four-cylinder Model 49 truck in 1915. GMC was one of many truck manufacturers to benefit from World War I. Production soared from hundreds to thousands of trucks each year. After the war, GM broadened its line to include light trucks by merging with the Chicago-based Yellow Cab Manufacturing Company. This was an important move. Today, light truck sales are an important component of the GMC strategy. On the eve of the Great Depression, GM positioned itself to be a major car and truck manufacturer by constructing a sprawling plant in Pontiac, Michigan. During this period, GM purchased Vauxhall in England, Adam Opel AG in Germany, and Holdens in Australia. In 1924, GM assembled its first vehicles abroad in Denmark.

This bold-looking GMC cab-over carries custom cars and street rods cross-country for California Street Rods.

This 1948 A Model GMC had a 671 Detroit Diesel under its hood and pulled for Parker Truck Company of San Diego, California.

An 860 series GMC, circa 1958, is loaded with machinery in this 1965 picture taken near Toledo, Ohio.

GMC helped promote the need for paved roads and cross-country travel. It had taken the Warwicks, a husband and wife team, a whopping two months to drive a GMC Model 31 from Seattle to New York in 1916, but they were the first to complete the grueling trip by car. Safety emerged as an issue, and GM responded in 1926 with shatter-resistant glass. In a 1927 publicity stunt, GMC hired race driver Cannonball Baker to drive a two-ton tanker filled with ocean water from New York to San Francisco. He did it in just under six days. The message was clear: better roads could connect the nation in the same way that railroads had in the previous century. Of course, GMC had a vested interest in encouraging the nation to build roads. The industrial giant was about to become the most popular truck.

In 1927, GMC launched the T series. The T-95, first built in 1931, was one of the first Class 8 rigs. It was designed like a semi with three axles, air brakes, and a four-speed transmission. GM also built trailers in order to survive the 1930s. The company was not conservative during the hard economic times. In 1934, it introduced a cab-over model. And it helped the country bounce back from the Depression in the late 1930s with new streamlined designs that

Buz Shoemaker's 1952 900 series "Jimmy" gets ready to unload some hay that was loaded near Indio, California. A 238-horsepower Detroit Diesel, backed by a five-speed main and three-speed auxiliary transmission, got this rig down the road.

A 1959 GMC "Cannonball" cab-over with integral sleeper is seen here pulling for Berger Moving. At the time (1965), Berger was an agent for Global Van Lines. Today, Berger is an Allied Van Lines agent.

looked particularly good on its now colorful trucks. GMC's Chevrolet truck plant came on line in Oakland in 1937.

The A series truck appeared before World War II. And GM, which had used Buick and GMC six-cylinder engines, began to experiment with diesel truck engines. GMC is most remembered for its DUKW "Duck" amphibian truck during World War II, but the corporation produced a wide range of vehicles—more than one-half million in all. GM's Adam Opel AG facility in Germany had been a leading producer during the 1930s. But in 1939 GM withdrew from Germany as John Smith explained, in response to allegations by the *Washington Post*:

Another GMC cab-over, circa 1958, is pulling a set of feed trailers for Leonard Van Der Linden of Artesia, California.

This 1965 photo taken in Perrysburg, Ohio, shows a new GMC "Crackerbox" cab-over with an integral sleeper. This model was quite popular with both the freight lines and steel haulers in the Midwest.

ALTHOUGH THE UNITED STATES WAS STILL NEUTRAL IN 1939, AFTER WAR BROKE OUT IN EUROPE, GM RECOGNIZED THAT THE NAZIS WOULD WANT TO CONVERT THE OPEL MANUFACTURING FACILITIES TO MAKE PRODUCTS FOR THE GERMAN WAR EFFORT. GM DID NOT WANT ITS AMERICAN PERSONNEL TO PARTICIPATE IN THE PRODUCTION OF PRODUCTS DESTINED FOR GERMANY'S USE IN THE WAR. THIS LED TO GENERAL MOTORS' WITHDRAWAL IN 1939 OF ITS AMERICAN EXECUTIVES . . . THE LAST AMERICAN EMPLOYEE ASSIGNED TO OPEL LEFT GERMANY IN EARLY MARCH 1941 . . . WHEN GERMANY DECLARED WAR ON THE UNITED STATES . . . , THE GENERAL MOTORS RELATIONSHIP WITH OPEL WAS SEVERED COMPLETELY. WE ARE UNAWARE OF ANY FORCED LABOR BEING USED AT THE OPEL FACILITIES WHILE AMERICAN PERSONNEL HAD OPERATING CONTROL . . . (STATEMENT, DECEMBER 14, 1998).

During World War II, President Roosevelt appointed GM's president William S. Knudsen to the National Defense Advisory Council as lieutenant general for War Department production. GM was America's largest defense contractor. It built airplane engines, airplanes and parts, tanks, marine diesels, guns, shells, and of course, trucks. The period between 1945 and 1949 is highlighted by the famous A Model truck.

After the war, GMC moved forward with its plans for diesel engine trucks. Its six-cylinder, 225-horsepower "Million Miler" moved the H Model during the 1950s. It was now the company's only Class 8 rig. GM did offer bubblenose cab-over and sleeper options to keep pace with the competition. This truck featured a prominent radiator grille capped with a GMC nameplate, fender mounted headlights, a two-piece angled windshield, and a slender rounded hood. GM introduced curved windshields that increased driver vision and reduced glare.

General Motors Corporation celebrated its fiftieth anniversary in 1958. From 1959 to 1967, GM switched to a square "cracker-box" cab-over model. The two-piece windshield was larger and more upright; the grille was nearly lost in the bumper; headlights were recessed; and the fenders were adorned with square covers. This was replaced by the Astro 95. The redesigned cab-over, offered in sleeper and nonsleeper versions, became the basis for a wide range of improvements. The Astro 95 hailed a return to a more rounded cab-over look, and a return of a more prominent grille; but GM now retained the oversized windshield by adding wraparound windshields. GM used larger wraparound windshields and larger radiators. Like

The GMC Astro was first introduced in 1968 and was well received. Seen here at a Santa Rosa, California, truck show, an Astro is set up to carry petroleum.

This particular model GMC was perfect for city use, where tight turns made deliveries difficult.

most successful truck manufacturers, GM used aluminum to reduce the weight of the trucks and make them more fuel efficient. By now, GM was among some 200 truck companies with postwar global operations. It continued to be safety conscious by assisting in the development of concrete bridge rails in 1962—an innovation adopted throughout the United States for use in medians.

GM also redesigned its conventional truck although it retained its long hood. The H Model was replaced by the 9500 series in 1966. The company offered a Detroit Diesel V-12 engine.

GMC Overview

Today, General Motors Corporation continues to be a major manufacturer of American automobiles and light trucks. Consumer models such as the Sierra and Sonoma pickups and the Suburban are popular. GMC also finances cars, trucks, businesses, and homes through the General Motors Acceptance Corporation (GMAC). Automobile financing accounts for about 40 percent of GMAC revenues from its

This GMC Brigadier is pulling for United Van Lines. This single-axle (one rear axle) was seen at a Las Vegas truck stop in 1988.

In the 1980s, Las Vegas Paving Company had an entire fleet of these GMC Generals. This model was built until the early 1990s, when production ceased.

Bob Pielemeier ran this 1966 long-hood GMC from Los Angeles to Phoenix, hauling produce. Pielemeier was a loyal client of GMC trucks.

730 worldwide offices. GM's largest overseas expansion project came in 1981 when it opened a European assembly plant in Zaragoza, Spain.

AN INDUSTRY GIANT

General Motors Corporation is an industry giant that was greatly affected by deregulation and restructuring of the 1980s and 1990s. "American firms were forced to adjust to increased global competition even though it required the closure of many factories and massive layoffs," said chairman John Smith. The company's GMC Truck Internet site explains its continued commitment to trucks:

> TRUCKS AREN'T SOMETHING WE DO AS A HOBBY. THEY'VE BEEN OUR SOLE PURPOSE FOR NEARLY 100 YEARS. WHEN YOU ARE THAT SINGLE-MINDED, THAT COMMITTED TO ONE THING, YOU LEARN WHAT IT TAKES TO DO IT WELL. YOU LEARN FROM EXPERIENCE TO STAY TRUE TO WHAT YOU KNOW ABOUT TRUCKS, AND ABOUT THE DEMANDS OF THE PEOPLE WHO USE THEM.

The GMC nameplate is prominent on consumer trucks such as the Sierra, but to find a Class 8 truck today, you need to look elsewhere.

THE VOLVO-WHITE-GMC-AUTOCAR FAMILY

A 1988 merger led GMC to join forces with the Volvo-White truck group. The group holds the nameplates for Volvo, White, GMC, and Autocar. Volvo is by far the most common nameplate on Class 8 rigs produced by this group. It experienced an amazing 22 percent growth in North American truck sales between 1998 and 1999, selling more than 23,000. North American sales accounted for slightly more than half of Volvo global truck sales in 1999.

Volvo carries on the GMC tradition of thinking globally. For example, Volvo trucks supply D12 engines from Brazil to an assembly plant in Belgium. Sales have increased dramatically in Western Europe as well as in North America. "We have invested considerable resources in ensuring that our production facilities are fully interchangeable," said Volvo Truck president Sten-Ake Aronsson. Volvo introduced the NH truck in 1999, and it invested some $60 million in the Brazil operation.

Volvo truck operations began in 1928, and the company is rapidly becoming one of the world's leading heavy-duty truck manufacturers. The company sells in 120 markets, but Europe, North America, and South America are its focal points. Company president Karl-Erling Trogen said: "The company is extending its global presence by setting up new operations in growth markets such as Eastern Europe, India, and China." Volvo employs modular components that are used in a wide range of truck models: "This approach results in fewer components, a high level of flexibility in the industrial system, and the potential for customer adaptation," he said. Volvo says its core corporate values beyond profitability are quality, safety, and environmental concerns. Truck drivers have attested to Volvo's safety record. Following a 1999 crash that pushed his rig through 100 feet of guardrail and off a bridge, driver Todd Schultz said his truck landed hard on the roof: "If it weren't for the Volvo cab, I wouldn't be here today."

While Volvo has taken on the role as big-rig leader in the corporate family, GMC has settled into its automobile and light truck roots. GMC continues to be a popular nameplate for light trucks, but it is common to see a GMC tractor-trailer truck in service today. Occasionally you can spot a WhiteGMC nameplate on the nation's highways.

This GMC General in Everett, Washington, is picking up a load of material for a construction job. The GMCs proved themselves to be sturdy and dependable vehicles.

CHAPTER 9

WHITE TRUCKS

An early pioneer in steam-powered commercial vehicles, White ultimately gained a reputation for offering a wide range of basic and luxury trucks with interchangeable parts.

—Rob Wagner, truck historian (1997)

At first glance, it might to be difficult to fathom what a needle and thread has to do with the development of the American semi-truck. But then, you would have to have been around during the Civil War to know.

WHITE ORIGINS: SEWING THE INDUSTRIAL AGE

Thomas Howard White, George Baker, and D'Arcy Porter thought business was strong enough in Templeton, Massachusetts, in 1859 to start selling sewing machines. By 1866, they moved the expanding business to Cleveland. After tinkering with sewing machines, White's three sons developed an interest in cars and trucks. Like most mechanically minded people of the period, the sons saw a huge potential in motor cars. Surprisingly, it wasn't that much of a leap from sewing machines to motors. Walter White became president of the White Motor Company, which built two steam-powered pie wagons in 1900.

Walter's brother, Rollin, who oversaw manufacturing, won a gold medal at the St. Louis fair in 1905 for his design work on steam engines used in trucks called "Stanhopes." In 1910, White offered a three-ton gasoline truck. By 1911, White had joined the industry shift and phased out steam in favor of gasoline-powered engines. White used pneumatic tires on its pre–World War I commercial vehicles.

WHITE OVERVIEW

White was the United States Army's standard truck during World War I, and the production of 18,000 trucks sealed its future as a truck rather than car company. Many of the trucks entered private industry through Army surplus sales, and White trucks became popular among larger operators. The Model 59 truck introduced the six-cylinder era in 1928. It featured 100 horsepower and could carry a four-ton load. As the Great Depression hit, White absorbed the Indiana Truck Company. Walter White died in 1929.

White's 730 cab-over series built in 1934 boasted a twelve-cylinder engine. White came to be known as a truck of power with its "Superpower" side-valve gasoline engines. The 700 series trucks were replaced by the WA and WB trucks during the World War II era.

In 1937 White commissioned designer Count Alexis de Saknoffsky to style the Labatt's Beer truck from a Model 818 cab-over and matching rounded trailer. The Labatt's Beer truck was simply one

Terry Klenske of Dalton Trucking in Fontana, California, owns this neat-looking 1948 Autocar. It is pulling a set of 1961 Fruehauf trailers used for transporting powdered cement.

A 1986 White with an integral sleeper is seen here at a truck show. It has gone as far as Washington state to pick up and tow a truck back to Southern California for Jim's Towing of Costa Mesa.

In the early 1950s, the White 3000 series was one of the most popular trucks among long-haul truckers in the moving industry. Many of the early White 3000s were gasoline-powered, but the one with a sleeper in this 1967 picture in Tucson, Arizona had a diesel engine.

J. H. Rose Truck Line, of Texas, had an entire fleet of two-axle White Superpower tractors with small integral sleepers in the 1950s. They hauled oilfield equipment in the Southwest. This 1964 picture shows a three-axle White with a small sleeper box, leased to J. H. Rose. The basic color for the Rose fleet was bright red.

of the most stylish trucks built to that point. The truck had a buslike look that featured ahead-of-its-time aerodynamic styling. The attention to styling and form foreshadowed future truck designs.

INNOVATION IN OHIO

White introduced the WC series in 1949, offering a diesel engine option and an integral sleeper cab. The company also introduced and briefly produced the Model 3000, a rounded cab-over model that was quite aerodynamic for its time. However, it was also quite expensive for its time. The Super Power 3000 featured power tilt cabs and air brakes. By 1951, the Cummins diesel engine was a regular option.

Perhaps White's most significant contribution to trucking was its acquisition of the well-known nameplates Freightliner and Sterling in 1951, and Autocar in 1953. The modern era for White is marked in 1957 by the purchase of Reo Motors, which led to the purchase in

This 1964 picture shows a White, circa 1957, working for Sanchez Trucking of Albuquerque, New Mexico. The 35-foot reefer trailer once belonged to Hutchinson Fruit & Produce. Notice the Kenworth sleeper on this rig.

The 5000 series White, shown in Ohio in this 1965 photo, was not a good-looking truck, but it proved that fiberglass was starting to come of age in the cab construction of Class 8 trucks.

1958 of Diamond T trucks. White merged Diamond T and Reo into the Diamond Reo nameplate in 1960. The White family had managed to keep several nameplates going. Windsor White, who had led the early marketing efforts of the company, died in 1959. White struggled to find its market, offering the Cummins diesel and its Mustang gasoline engines with as much as 215 horsepower. Eventually, gasoline engines would be phased out, but not before some trucks were offered with a Chevrolet V-8. White's Model TDs were fairly standard-styled semis, featuring both one- and two-piece windshields, and various configurations of bumpers, headlights, and grilles.

White began to falter with the introduction of its innovative Model 5000, produced from 1959 to 1962. It had a two-piece teardrop windshield, a modern-looking cab-over design, and dual headlights. But its fiberglass construction, though light, was weak, and the doors leaked! It was a sad period in the company history, marked by the death of the last and most important of the White brothers, Rollin, in 1962.

Truckers often refer to the 7000 series White as "The Japanese Freightliner." It received a warmer response than did the previous Model 5000, and annual sales figures proved it.

The Lincoln Highway

Carl Fisher, who helped originate the Indianapolis Motor Speedway in 1909, and was its president, had an idea in 1912. If the federal government would build a transcontinental highway, then the states might just build more and better roads. He named the project the Lincoln Highway to give it a patriotic sound. President Taft agreed that such a project would help build national unity, and construction began in 1914. A highway stretching from Jersey City, New Jersey, to San Francisco, California—3,385 miles—was a major undertaking. Today, you will find the old Lincoln Highway along U.S. 30. Fisher went on to finance the building of Miami Beach, and he owned an automobile dealership in Indianapolis.

The Lincoln Highway began along existing dirt and gravel roads in just 13 states, but by 1924 it was part of a federal highway network. Route 30, as it came to be known, was completed in 1935 when the last bit of it was paved in Nebraska. Today, Omahans know the roadway as Dodge Street—an east-west main street through the center of town.

The Lincoln Highway Association, formed in 1992, has sparked renewed interest in the road that helped move the nation. With the road in place, trucking emerged as a major economic force. The Lincoln Highway was the harbinger of the interstate highway system, and it showed the nation that goods could be moved quickly and efficiently along roadways. If you follow the Lincoln Highway's path today, you can see the Watson "1733 Ranch" in Kearney, Nebraska—named as the halfway point between Boston and San Francisco: "The ranch is gone but a large road sign remains to mark the spot that is, arguably, the very middle of the United States," writes Midwest Living. Today, many museums dot the trail of the old Lincoln Highway, but you will need to exit Interstate 80 to see the sites!

(**Sources:** *The World Book Encyclopedia*, 1960; "A road trip to remember; Driving Nebraska's old Lincoln Highway," *Midwest Living* Nebraska Traveler, 1999.)

A late-1970s White cab-over is seen here with a load of lumber near Eureka, California, circa 1976.

This 1980s White had a drom box behind its sleeper for carrying extra payload. Drom boxes are especially popular with many "bedbug" haulers.

White turned to aluminum for its Model 7000, available in sleeper and nonsleeper cabs. Operators of the period called it "the Japanese Freightliner." The Model 7000 was a sturdy, more conventional cab-over. It featured prominent chrome bumpers and rounded corner plates. It returned White to a single headlight configuration, flat and oval two-piece windshields, and a simple grille just below the White nameplate. It had a boxy-looking cab.

White offered other models such as the Road Commander during the 1970s, and the company continued to offer conventional trucks such as the 4000 and 9000 series. White's Road Boss was a conventional truck with a prominent nose and large "W H I T E" lettering. A chrome bumper and single headlamp design, as well as a tall one-piece windshield, gave it a sturdy and powerful image. However, White placed too much faith in the possibility of returning Cummins diesel engines back to gasoline—naming them "Mustang" and "White Giesel"—just as the government was cracking down on engine emissions.

continued on page 104

Art Van Beek owns El Monte Dairy in Tipton, California. His 1952 Autocar with its 1944 Weber three-axle trailer is used to haul hay from Nevada into Art's dairy on a regular basis.

Autocars were designed for severe service, and this unit is in the sugarcane fields of Kauai in 1975. The motoring public seldom sees trucks like this because they are used in off-highway situations.

ABOVE RIGHT: *In Tucson in 1967, a 1950s Autocar poses long enough for a picture. Autocars were not a common truck for the moving industry.*

RIGHT: *This 1960 Autocar was the pride of the Kings County fleet of milk haulers. It was driven and maintained by "Fatso" Pierce, who always kept it in mint condition.*

Francis Mooney of Dillon, Montana, carried produce with this neat dark blue and white Autocar. It is seen here in 1965 loading produce at the old Jack Walker produce dock on Alameda Street in Los Angeles.

An Autocar with an integral sleeper is shown in this 1965 picture. The load of steel on board is the same kind of load that fell on photographer Stan Holtzman on March 4, 1964, while he helped load a 1947 Peterbilt and 35-foot flatbed trailer. Holtzman had an out-of-body experience and was laid up for over a year . . . a hell of a way to avoid going to Vietnam.

This 1960s Autocar logging truck is pictured in 1978 near Eureka, California. Autocars were a favorite among logging operators in Northern California, Oregon, Washington, and Canada.

Continued from page 101

White expansion with new plants in Virginia and Ohio led to the manufacture of models such as The Road Boss 2 in 1977 and the Autocar Construcktor 2 in 1978, but this was the wrong time to be making large investments. In 1980, White filed for Chapter 11 bankruptcy, and the new Volvo-White Corporation emerged in 1981. By the end of the 1980s, Volvo and General Motors had struck a deal. Volvo, GM, and Autocar were now under the same corporate umbrella with White, and the WhiteGMC nameplate still has some popularity. Nevertheless, the legacy of the White brothers today lives mostly through North American sales of Volvo trucks, as little is left of the empire built from a father's dream to sell sewing machines.

LEFT: *Pictured in downtown Boston, this 1980s Autocar is pulling for James Grant Demolition Company. Its large radiator indicates that something powerful lies under its hood.*

LOWER LEFT: *Nevada Power Company operates this 1984 Autocar. With its all-steel diamond-plate fenders and all-wheel drive, this unit is designed for some very severe working conditions.*

BELOW: *This is the way the current Autocar looks. Besides the Autocar nameplate that appears on the sides of the hood, the names White/GMC are also visible. Will the Autocar be phased out in the future? Only time will tell.*

Joe and Lorie Szirovicza lease this sharp-looking Volvo to Clark Moving & Storage of Rochester, New York. The long wheelbase and unusual sleeper makes this truck stand out from the rest.

An early-1990s Volvo makes up part of the fleet of trucks run by Ralphs Grocery Company in Los Angeles. Ralph's is one of the largest grocery chains in Southern California and has more trucks in its fleet than many trucking companies.

A Volvo/White/GMC cab-over is seen here with a set-back front axle for easier turning radius.

The diagonal strip running through the front grille is Volvo's trademark for its automobiles as well as its trucks. This cab-over is owned by a local beer distributor from Reno, Nevada.

Brooks & Dunn brings this late-model Volvo to various public functions and gatherings. Here it is seen at the Mid-America Truck Show in Louisville, Kentucky, in 1998.

CHAPTER 10

DODGE TRUCKS

Think of all the Ford owners who will someday want an automobile.
—John Dodge (circa 1914)

Buying Dodge was one of the soundest acts of my life.
—Walter Chrysler (1938)

The story of Dodge trucks sheds light on how all forms of early manufacturing impacted the development of the truck—including railroad locomotives and the bicycle. At the same time, it is also a story of how the American entrepreneurial spirit, production, and marketing know-how converged.

There were no motor-driven carriages in 1875 when Walter P. Chrysler was born in Wamego, Kansas. The son of a passenger railroad engineer on the Kansas Pacific Railroad, young Walter "loved to ride over the plains beside his father in the cab of the snorting iron juggernaut." According to company documents, he also loved the roundhouse, where skilled mechanics repaired locomotives. He learned to fight back when the bigger boys bullied him, and he sold milk from the family farm for a commission from his mother. As Walter grew up to become tall and husky, he dreamed of becoming a railroad mechanic.

It was 1892. Hundreds of miles away, in Springfield, Massachusetts, the first successful gasoline motor engine was powering a car. Walter was 17 when he became a railroad mechanic's apprentice. As he moved up through the ranks, he sent question after question on mechanical issues to *Scientific American*. The motor car industry was well underway in 1908, when at age 33, Walter Chrysler

suddenly became interested. He attended the Chicago Auto show. He took his life savings of $700 and borrowed another $4,300 to purchase a Locomobile, just so he could take it apart and study how it worked. Two years later he was working for Buick in Detroit, and within five years he had moved from a $6,000-per-year management job to the position of president and general manager—titles that earned him $500,000 at General Motors.

DODGE ORIGINS: VENTURING FROM DETROIT INTO THE FUTURE

As the twentieth century dawned, brothers John and Horace Dodge were busy building bicycles at their dad's machine shop. The family moved to Ontario, Canada, and the automobile industry at the time was full of hope and potential. By 1901, they were supplying parts for Oldsmobiles. John and Horace seemed to have a keen ability to grasp design and construction, and they soon came to the attention of none other than Henry Ford. He was so impressed with the Dodge boys that he offered them a one-tenth share in his new company in exchange for their expertise in building motors and transmissions. The partnership held for 12 years, and early Ford cars and trucks were built

A Canadian Dodge is seen in this 1988 picture taken in Las Vegas. This unusual-looking truck was last seen in Bakersfield, California, several years later.

Dan Kelly's Dodge Bighorn tractor with a Kenworth sleeper is shown in this 1996 picture. The Dodge Bighorn is truly a collector's item, as fewer than 200 were built between 1973–75.

with virtually all Dodge parts. In 1914, the Dodge brothers left Ford to have design freedom and formed Dodge Brothers, Incorporated. Dodge built 249 rugged cars named "Old Betsy."

The Maxwell Motor Company of Detroit competed with Dodge in the early days of the twentieth century:

> MAXWELL HAD BEEN A RESPECTED NAME IN THE AUTOMOTIVE WORLD. JONATHON DIXON MAXWELL, ONE OF THE TRUE PIONEERS OF THE INDUSTRY, HAD COLLABORATED WITH ELWOOD HAYNES IN BUILD-ING THE FIRST HAYNES CAR, BACK IN 1894. TEN YEARS LATER, HE FOUNDED THE MAXWELL MOTOR CAR COMPANY, INC.

According to *Chrysler Corporation, The Story of an American Company* (1955), Maxwell built a one-ton, four-cylinder truck in 1917, a year in which the company was ranked sixth in United States automobile production. But Maxwell had financial difficulties and a legal dispute with the Chalmers Motor Company over property leases. By 1920, Maxwell owed creditors more than $25 million. Walter Chrysler chaired the Maxwell-Chalmers Managing and Reorganization Committee. Chrysler was available because he had left General Motors a year earlier over disagreements with William Durant, the maverick president of GM. Chrysler had come out of his millionaire retirement to repair the financially troubled

The Dodge cab-overs from 1964 to around 1975 were well received by the trucking industry, especially by van lines. Few are seen on the highways today.

Willys-Overland company. His wealth placed him in a position to lead a group that pumped $15 million into Maxwell and paid creditors two-thirds of what was owed. Walter Chrysler was paid $100,000 per year plus valuable stock options at a time when he was used to earning $1 million a year for his skills. Chrysler hired three talented engineers—Fred Zeder, Owen Skelton, and Carl Breer—to move into a vacant Chalmers plant and begin designing a quality car that would bear his name. In 1925, he formed what would become the Chrysler Corporation under a plan to transfer Maxwell Motor Corporation stock, valued at $400 million.

DODGE OVERVIEW

During World War I, Dodge was building trucks, and the young company delivered nearly 20,000 vehicles to the military. Dodge Brothers had become one of the largest and most respected companies, and they were third among car manufacturers. Unexpectedly, both John and Horace died in 1920. For five years, heirs operated the meteoric company, and Dodge continued to grow while providing engines for Graham Brothers trucks. In 1925 a New York investment firm bought Dodge for $146 million. By 1927, Dodge had bought out an Indiana truck manufacturing operation and began using only the Dodge nameplate on its trucks. "But managing a big auto company is a specialized and exacting job," Chrysler Corporation would later write, "and within three years the bankers approached Walter Chrysler and suggested he buy them out." This would not be a hostile takeover. Chrysler moved slowly, and he insisted that 90 percent of Dodge stockholders accept the plan. He used more than one million shares of Chrysler stock valued at $80 per share, and he assumed $59 million of Dodge debt.

This set the stage for the signing of the papers on July 30, 1928. Chrysler executives immediately moved into the Dodge plant now adorned with the sign "Chrysler Corporation, Dodge Division." Walter Chrysler was doing the impossible. One observer said it was like "a minnow swallowing a whale." Still, in just 12 months, Walter Chrysler had launched two new auto lines—Plymouth and DeSoto—and he had "bought out and absorbed a rival company three times its size." For Walter Chrysler, the move placed him at the center of not only the automobile industry, but also the growing truck market. According to the company:

DODGE BROTHERS' TRUCKS (ORIGINALLY BUILT BY GRAHAM BROTHERS AND KNOWN AS GRAHAM BROTHERS TRUCKS) WERE ACCEPTED FOR RUGGEDNESS AND STAMINA. THE DODGE DEALER BODY WAS ONE OF THE STRONGEST IN THE INDUSTRY. MOREOVER, THE MAIN DODGE PLANT IN NEARBY HAMTRAMCK, A MUNICIPALITY INSIDE DETROIT, WAS ONE OF THE LARGEST AND MOST COMPLETELY INTEGRATED AUTOMOBILE FACTORIES IN THE WORLD, COVERED 58 ACRES AND EMPLOYED APPROXIMATELY 20,000 WORKERS. ITS FACILITIES WOULD PERMIT CHRYSLER CORPORATION TO EXERCISE ITS FULL MANUFACTURING POWER AND TALENTS.

During the 1930s sales soared and Dodge adorned its trucks with the ram hood ornament. Dodge-Chrysler was yet another company to benefit from World War II. Its Power Wagon helped build a reputation with people looking for rugged vehicles after the war. By 1936, Chrysler Corporation produced more than one million cars and trucks a year—nearly one-fourth of the nation's total production. Two years later, Walter Chrysler fell ill, and he died in 1940. Unlike a lot of companies of the period, however, Chrysler had built a management team that could carry on without him. K. T. Keller had been elected president in 1935, and he was prepared to guide the mammoth corporation as chief executive. "I liked Keller's looks the first time I saw him," Chrysler had said before his death. "He had the same love for machines that dominated my life."

Chrysler Corporation built a whopping 438,000 army trucks during World War II. During the 1940s, Dodge used the phrase "Job-Rated" for trucks sold in the commercial market. Chrysler struggled through shortages of raw materials after the war, but the company managed to revive civilian production of cars and trucks—676,000 in 1946, and 1.4 million by 1951. By the 1950s Chrysler was a billion dollar company that operated 54 plants. By the 1960s, Dodge's identification with the public was clearly as a car company, featuring classic models such as the 1950 Wayfarer Sportabout, the 1954 Royal 500 convertible, and the 1966 Charger. However, trucks such as the L Series and Bighorn helped keep the Dodge name familiar to truckers.

The L Series was introduced in 1964, offering a Class 8 tractor with a Cummins engine. The cab-over design was offered in sleeper and nonsleeper models. The classic and simple look of the L Series featured a flat, two-piece windshield, a box-shaped cab, simple recessed headlights, a subtle grille, and D O D G E chrome lettering. The L Series, popular with the moving industry (van lines), was discontinued in 1975.

LIFE OF THE BIGHORN

Dodge had planned to stay in the heavy truck market with the introduction of the Bighorn in the early 1970s, but only 261 Bighorns were produced when Dodge ceased production in 1975. Nevertheless, the Bighorn symbol continues to be important in Dodge's light truck sales today.

Dodge uses a Cummins 24-valve Turbo diesel in its Dodge Ram 2500 HD and 3500 pickups. Its so-called "Big Red Truck" is fashioned from a Dodge Ram 3500 Quad Cab 4x4, and it can pull 11,000 pounds. But DaimlerChrysler, Dodge's newest parent company, is deep into the heavy truck market with Freightliner, Sterling, and Mercedes-Benz brand names. Freightliner is the leading North American Class 8 truck producer, and the Portland, Oregon, company produces Class 6, 7, and 8 trucks throughout North America. The Sterling name is synonymous with delivery, construction, and long-hauling, and the Mercedes-Benz heavy trucks are very popular in Europe. Still, John and Horace Dodge left their mark on motor vehicles, and they helped make trucking what it is today. And Walter Chrysler emphasized the importance of design and engineering, a love for how things work, and a willingness to take financial risks in the interest of building a better truck.

CHAPTER 11

DIAMOND T

By the late 1950s, Diamond T was in trouble.
—Stan Holtzman, author and photographer (1995)

At the beginning of the twentieth century, it was difficult not to catch the excitement of the new motor car industry. The son of a Chicago "shoe dog" helped turn this interest into a commercial truck business.

DIAMOND T ORIGINS: A WINDY CITY PRODUCTION

Charles A. Tilt began building cars in 1905. One day, a few years later, one of his customers asked for a truck to haul plumbing supplies. Wanting the business, Tilt agreed and launched a line of trucks. The first Diamond T was a conventional four-cylinder one-and-a-half ton truck.

Tilt's father had made Diamond Brand shoes under a green diamond trademark with a gold border and a T inside. The T stood for Tilt. The diamond meant quality. C. A.'s challenge was to take Diamond T trucks from a fledgling local operation on the north side of Chicago to a major manufacturer able to meet the growing needs of a network of dealers stretching to both coasts. So, in 1916 Tilt purchased 14 acres on Chicago's southwest side and constructed a 250,000-square-foot plant. The jewel of this new facility was a 1,000-foot assembly line. During World War I, Tilt's new assembly lines produced 1,500 Series B "Liberty" trucks in just 18 months. Trucks were getting larger—three to five tons—and war fueled the new industry. Tested under extreme conditions, Diamond T built a reputation of quality that led to more government and civilian sales after the war.

DIAMOND OVERVIEW

In the days following the "war to end all wars," $2,000 or so would buy a four-cylinder, three-speed commercial truck with the latest features—pneumatic tires, front bumpers, and even radiator guards. Diamond T was considered a design leader in the use of chrome, molding, and running boards. Sales soared in the booming economy of the 1920s. Diamond T helped pioneer gas tankers for Texaco and by 1933 had introduced steel roof cabs, skirted fenders, and flashy grilles. An innovative tanker was featured at the Chicago World's Fair— "A Century of Progress" held June through October of 1933. Mayor Edward Kelly said that Chicagoans had been lucky to witness "the dawn of civilization's golden century of scientific and industrial achievement." It was a fair that allowed visitors to see GM automobiles being built and to test-drive a Chrysler. C. A. Tilt's spirit of optimism was fitting in a Windy City excited by the promise of the industrial age.

A Model 921 Diamond T with a small integral sleeper at a Washington truck show, put on by the American Truck Historical Society based in Alabama.

This Diamond T, circa 1948, is a single-axle tractor from Stockton, California. The late 1940s were good years for Diamond T, as truckers on both sides of the country liked them.

Diamond T's innovation continued in the 1930s with a new V-windshield tilted at a 30 degree angle. C. A. Tilt was said to be a hands-on leader who pushed the company to keep changing its truck designs. As Diamond T continued to build large trucks, it also entered the lucrative small-truck market. In the years before World War II, Diamond T's grille and hood chrome became flashy.

Diamond T built 10-ton trucks for heavy hauling, and the company introduced its first cab-over model in 1937. The taller cabs still featured a somewhat conventional grille. When the United States entered World War II and diesel became a fuel of choice, Diamond T, along with all other truck manufacturers of the period, shifted gears.

Overall, Diamond T produced about 50,000 trucks, including more than 6,000 12-ton tank tractors. They pulled 12-wheel trailers with loaded gross weights of as much as 80 tons. Once again, the company used a world war to show its strengths and was poised to sell large numbers of civilian trucks in the postwar economy. C. A. Tilt

Tom Smith of Cottonwood, California, ran this 1948 Diamond T up until the 1980s, hauling whatever he could fit in his trailer.

A young kid with his dad checks out this restored 1948 Model 209 Diamond T at a 1989 truck show in Ontario, California.

moved from president to board chairman in 1946. When the company peaked in 1948, its Chicago plant featured nine buildings, producing 10,651 trucks.

Diamond T partnered with International in 1950 to build what was called the "comfort cab." They achieved fuel economy by bringing outside air into the engine compartment. Diamond T also introduced its largest trucks built at the Chicago plant—the 950 and 951 series. The 950 was targeted at the growing western truck market, where power was essential.

By 1951, Diamond T decided to focus on large trucks. Its tilt cab-over-engine design won a national award for the 723C. The cab design was also used on International trucks, and it became a model for other COEs.

An August 1965 truck inspection, held by the Ohio State Patrol, temporarily stops this Reo Comet south of the Ohio Turnpike at Exit 5. The Reo Comet was one of the best selling Reo trucks ever made.

This "Blue Goose" appears to be a 1955 model and has a small factory sleeper that provided little room to move around. The trailer is a 40-foot "pot" or "possum-belly" that allows for more livestock to be transported.

Joe Alegria's 1956 Diamond T livestock truck and trailer. At one time the trailer pulled for Roscoe Wagner of Twin Falls, Idaho. Besides hauling livestock, Roscoe Wagner was a successful Wilson Trailer dealer in Idaho, and though Roscoe is deceased, his brother Roger is at the helm, carrying on the Wagner tradition.

In this 1965 picture taken in Michigan, a Brada Miller truck is seen running across a set of scales, with its load of steel coils. The tractor is a Diamond T, circa 1955.

When C. A. Tilt died in 1956, his company could not survive independently. Just two years later, White Motor Company purchased Diamond T. White had owned Reo Motors for three years and moved Diamond's production to Lansing, Michigan, in 1961. Diamond T production continued separately for a time but was strongly influenced now by White and its conventional cabs. The D cab featured a wraparound split windshield. The R cab was a single sheet of curved glass. Diamond T's last model was built in 1966. It was a tilt cab-over HF3000 called the "Trend." Manufactured from lightweight plastic, it was ahead of its time—perhaps too ahead of its time.

DIAMOND REO

White merged Diamond and Reo—two lines it had homogenized at Lansing for more than five years—into the Diamond Reo nameplate in 1967, but it spun off the new group a year later because of financial struggles. Diamond Reo production peaked with 9,136 trucks in 1974.

Continuing financial problems, however, led to bankruptcy in 1975. The truck manufacturer had struggled through some of the

This Diamond T, parked in Wyoming in 1965, is pulling for Glenn Smith & Sons, a petroleum distributor in Wyoming. The tractor appears to be a 1956 model.

This Missouri-based Diamond T, circa 1957, is shown in a 1994 picture. It is used to haul pools and spas in the "Show Me" State.

This massive Diamond T was seen at an Oregon truck show and was one of the largest tractors ever produced for on-highway use. It sat as high as many cab-overs and is a rare sight today.

Jerry Noordman's 1961 Model 931 was one of many Diamond Ts owned by Dunkley Distributing Company of Salt Lake City, Utah. The truck was fully restored and now resides with Jerry in Enumclaw, Washington. Power is supplied by a supercharged Cummins 320-horsepower engine, backed by a five-speed main and four-speed auxiliary transmission.

slowest production years since the 1920s. Some 163 new trucks were sold off that fall. An Ohio firm continued to supply parts to the more than 200,000 Diamond T, Reo, and Diamond Reo trucks still on the road. In 1977 Diamond Reo landed in the hands of Osterlund, Incorporated, in Harrisburg, Pennsylvania. Diamond Reos continued to be built in the 1980s, but by 1993 Osterlund had sold. A new Diamond T company was formed, but truck manufacturing during the late 1990s became dominated by major multinational corporations. Diamond T ended production and sold out its remaining stock of trucks. Diamond T will be remembered most for the entrepreneurial spirit of C. A. Tilt in the 1920s, his continuous design changes in the 1930s, and the prominent role Diamond T played during the 1940s and 1950s. In the end, it can be said that Diamond T was Tilt's company. It could not prosper without him.

This 1960s Diamond T cab-over was parked behind Shorty Campbell's Truck Stop in Rosemead, California, in 1967.

Circle M Trucking of Los Angeles ran this Diamond T cab-over in the 1960s. It was rare to see a rig like this set up as a dump truck with pup trailer.

Leroy Beach of Hamilton, Texas, hauled cattle with this Diamond T cab-over. This picture was taken in Tucson, Arizona, in 1963.

In this 1966 picture, a new Diamond T is seen pulling for Market Express of Fresno, California.

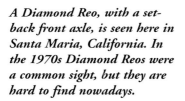

A Diamond Reo, with a setback front axle, is seen here in Santa Maria, California. In the 1970s Diamond Reos were a common sight, but they are hard to find nowadays.

CHAPTER 12

OTHER NOTABLE NAME PLATES

Built to Last.
—Hayes trucks (circa 1969)

The evolution of the American semi-truck is partly reflected in the nameplates that no longer grace our highways or that have small roles in trucking today. Many of the nation's most interesting trucks were built by companies that are gone but not forgotten. Other truck companies remain but have relatively small operations.

AMERICAN COLEMAN

G. L. Coleman of Omaha, Nebraska, founded a truck company in 1923. After some initial design work, he moved to Littleton, Colorado, and began production in 1925. He designed the earliest 4x4, 6x4, and 6x6 trucks as state highway and military trucks. By 1928, Coleman had introduced a seven-and-a-half ton truck for logging and oil hauling off-highway work. Coleman increased his early four-cylinder Buda engines to six, and he offered a four-speed Fuller transmission with an additional two-speed transmission. Coleman built 2- to 10-ton trucks and supplied crane carriers during World War II, but he faltered after the war. A paralyzing year-long labor dispute in 1949 destroyed Coleman's dealer network. Despite an air force contract in the early 1950s, he never made a full comeback.

The Coleman Space Star of 1968 was a four-wheel-drive tractor with an attached semi-trailer and an optional second four-wheel trailer. The Space Star had no fifth wheel. Instead, it had a unique system that allowed the truck frame to slide beneath a trailer and lock into place with eight pins. The result produced a single tractor-trailer unit that was more maneuverable, particularly because of a four-wheel steering system. The 318-horsepower Detroit Diesel featured speeds of up to 80 miles per hour, a roll-bar constructed cab, and adjustable

The name Studebaker is associated with cars that looked like rocket ships from an old Flash Gordon movie. However, here is proof that Studebaker was serious about making a long-distance truck.

Fageol was the predecessor to Peterbilt, and the Fageol seen here closely resembles the early Peterbilt.

American Coleman's one and only "Batmobile" is seen in this 1969 picture. The rig was far ahead of its time, incorporating dual sleepers, an engine that rolled out to be serviced, a tractor that locked into place to become part of the trailer (as in truck and trailer), and the option of two steering axles.

air suspension to match loading dock height. The cab-over slept one above and one behind the driver. Called "the Batmobile" for its forward-thinking aerodynamics, the prototype truck never caught on.

FAGEOL

In the cornfields of Iowa, twin brothers William and Frank Fageol built their first gasoline-powered motor car in 1899. They joined businessman Louis Bill in Oakland, California, and founded Fageol Motors in 1916. Fageol used parts from a wide range of companies and assembled trucks for navigating steep inclines. This California company introduced a cab-over-engine design in 1937, but the company never recovered from the Great Depression. In 1938, Fageol was sold to Sterling in Milwaukee, but truck production ended within a year. The manufacturing arm of the company was sold to T. A. Peterman, and he renamed the trucks Peterbilt.

HAYES

Two Canadians, Douglas Hayes and W. E. Anderson, formed the Hayes-Anderson Motor Company in Vancouver in 1920. They built a heavy-duty truck targeted at loggers. They were the first to switch to diesel-powered logging trucks in 1933. The company had been renamed Hayes Manufacturing in 1928, but the Hayes-Anderson nameplate survived through 1934. A 1946 merger with Lawrence Manufacturing broadened the company's off-highway offerings. In 1969, Mack Trucks purchased the Hayes operation but sold it just five years later to Gearmatic, a division of Paccar. Within a year, production under the Hayes nameplate ended. Hayes said its trucks were "Built to Last," and indeed, some remain on the job in oil fields and logging operations today.

An older Hayes sits in British Columbia. Some of the largest logging trucks ever built were Hayes trucks and are still in active service on Vancouver Island, although they are no longer built.

MARMON

A quality motor car company in the early 1900s, Marmon of Indianapolis built an automobile named the "Wasp" that won the first Indy 500 in 1911. At an average speed of just over 74 miles per hour, the race took driver Ray Harroun in car number 32 nearly seven hours to complete. Marmon shifted its focus to trucks as it struggled to survive the Great Depression. In 1963, Marmon was sold to Space, Incorporated, near Dallas, Texas.

Using the knowledge and expertise it acquired during World War II, Marmon built cab-over-engine models and added conventional models during the 1970s. First and foremost, Marmon was known as a "hand-crafted" truck built to last. Marmon trucks were built individually from hand-made cabs, sleepers, and chassis. The last Marmon was built in 1997, and thus marked the end of an era for a truly custom-built truck.

Marmon went out of business in 1997, marking the end of a non-mass-produced truck. Marmon not only made quality, custom-built trucks, but in the early 1930s, it made quality cars equal to Packard and Pierce Arrow.

Taken in Quesnel, British Columbia, this photo shows a 1980s Western Star loading wood chips. Western Stars, built in Canada, are the obvious truck of choice by many truckers.

Western Star trucks were, at one time, part of the White family of trucks. Note that White appears on this rig. This tractor appears to be a 1960s or early 1970s model.

A 1980s Western Star is shown in New England in 1988. Trucks in the East are famous for their pinstriping and gold-leaf lettering.

Besides building a conventional model, Marmon built cab-overs like this one in Reno, Nevada, in 1984. Marmons were made in Texas, and their factory now produces the massive International Paystar trucks.

STUDEBAKER

In 1852, Henry and Clem Studebaker started selling wagons to Indiana farmers. By the 1890s, the H&C Studebaker shop in South Bend was tinkering with the automobile. They built an electric car in 1902 and a gasoline-powered auto in 1904. The 1908 Studebaker Suburban was a forward-looking motor car with a removable seat for storage. After incorporation in 1911, Studebaker moved into truck manufacturing. Studebaker was in and out of truck and bus manufacturing until its 1928 acquisition of Pierce-Arrow and its 1932 investment in White and Indiana trucks. Production peaked in 1931 with 3,495 trucks, but the Great Depression led Studebaker to divest its interests in Pierce-Arrow, White, and Indiana trucks. Its T, K, and J series trucks were popular during the 1930s, but its M series in 1941 was a disaster. It was a heavy truck that was replaced by lighter and more powerful models—the 2R, 3R, and E series during the 1940s and 1950s. Truck production ended in 1965, and the company closed its doors just a year later.

A late-model Western Star Constellation is seen here at a Las Vegas truck stop. Dave and Carol Franzen of Nebraska run this rig coast-to-coast.

The famous dancing raisins of California can be seen across the trailer of this 1988 Western Star, owned by a trucker from Rockford, Illinois.

This Western Star is being washed in Oregon. Most Western Star owners take extra pride in their trucks.

Doug Gravel of Worthington, Iowa, maintains this clean Western Star. Doug runs from Iowa to the West Coast with this classic-looking rig.

Some new Western Stars are seen here at a Las Vegas dealership. The old wives' tale of Western Star trucks being heavier than their competitors is clearly just a myth.

WESTERN STAR

North America's only remaining hand-built trucks had one problem: they were heavy enough to be called "lead sleds" by some. But a 1998 lighter-weight design featuring aluminum and plastics created a new star. Western Star Trucks, Inc., is located in Kelowna, British Columbia, Canada. The company focuses on design and manufacture of "quality, highly customized, Class 8 heavy-duty trucks for both highway and vocational markets." Western Star's reputation is built on two goals: reliability and durability. Western Star was created by White Motor Company in 1967—a response to the demands of the American West Coast and Canadian markets. The first Class 8 Western Star trucks were built for logging and mining, as well as oil and gas exploration. During the 1970s, Western Star expanded into highway trucks. In 1981 two Calgary resource-based companies purchased the assets of White and changed the name of the company to Western Star Trucks, Inc.

In 1991, Australia-based Terrence E. Peabody incorporated Western Star Trucks Holdings Ltd. According to Western Star, the reorganization "dramatically improved the product development and manufacturing capabilities of the company." Growth during the 1990s led to stock offerings in Canada in 1994 and the United States in 1996. About the same time, Western Star purchased Orion Bus Industries and ERF Trucks. Western Star's 2 percent market share has, according to *Overdrive* magazine, given customers of the Constellation series "a sense of being part of an exclusive club, in which members waved at each other going down the road."

Western Star focuses on "premium, made-to-order heavy-duty trucks." The company reports:

WESTERN STAR, UNLIKE LARGE FLEET MARKET MANUFACTURERS, DESIGNS AND HAND BUILDS CUSTOMIZED, SHORT-PRODUCTION RUN VEHICLES AND OFFERS APPROXIMATELY 8,000 OPTIONS, INCLUDING DIFFERENT ENGINE, TRANSMISSION, AXLE, AND CHASSIS COMBINATIONS. THE COMPANY IS ONE OF THE FEW NORTH AMERICAN HEAVY-DUTY TRUCK ASSEMBLY LINES THAT ALSO BUILDS RIGHT-HAND DRIVE VEHICLES, A FLEXIBILITY THAT ALLOWS WESTERN STAR TO SELL TO AUSTRALIA, NEW ZEALAND, INDONESIA, AND OTHER RIGHT-HAND DRIVE MARKETS.

Western Star has more than 250 dealers. Its heavy-duty Heritage and Constellation Class 8 series trucks in North America, as well as Latin America, Africa, and the Middle East, helped the company

grow sales during the 1990s. Parts and service represent about one-third of average heavy truck operating costs, and Western Star has emphasized the creation and maintenance of a dealer network in North America:

A WESTERN STAR TRUCK REFLECTS LEGENDARY QUALITY, CRAFTSMANSHIP, AND ATTENTION TO DETAIL. IT'S NOT JUST ANOTHER PRODUCTION LINE VEHICLE. FOR OVER 30 YEARS WESTERN STAR HAS HAND BUILT TRUCKS EXACTLY TO THE DEMANDING SPECIFICATIONS OF OUR CUSTOMERS. WE UNDERSTAND THE PRIDE IN OWNING A WESTERN STAR. WHETHER YOU'RE AN OWNER-OPERATOR OR FLEET OWNER, OUR SUPERIOR ENGINEERING, RELIABILITY AND STEP-BY-STEP QUALITY CONTROL KEEPS EACH WESTERN STAR RUNNING BETTER AND HOLDING ITS VALUE LONGER.

Dependability and performance are the goals of Western Star trucks. Drivers and owner operators agree that this truck breaks rank with the rest of the pack. So, keep a look out for the next Star.

This Western Star, circa 1984, has enough chrome and pinstriping to gain anyone's attention. This unit ran from Wisconsin to the West Coast transporting refrigerated commodities.

CHAPTER 13

TRUCK SHOWS
LEARNING FROM THE PAST

In my eyes, all the trucks are winners, whether they are in shows,
just working out on the road, or retired to the bone yard
after giving a full life of service.

—Linda Johnson, Pride & Polish Manual (1996)

I f you see a trucker standing proudly next to a freshly polished rig, something special may be in the air. Drivers and owner-operators who see themselves as dedicated professionals can compete in a wide range of categories at truck shows. Out on the interstate, it is fairly common to come across a truck featuring custom pinstripes, elaborately painted trailers, and creative names such as "Wilderness Dream," "Streaker," or "Western Spirit."

INDOOR AND OUTDOOR EVENTS

Truck shows fall into two categories: indoor and outdoor. Of course, indoor events make sense when the weather is very hot or very cold. Also, artificial lighting makes the trucks look flashier. Paint and chrome seem to display greater shine inside a large building. Truck shows held in newer buildings feature user-friendly facilities and air conditioning. The truck show is a place for truck manufacturers to display their newest product lines, and they want clients to be comfortable. Children love seeing the big rigs, and they often join adults in marveling at the size and power of today's trucks. Manufacturers, seeking to lure business, see their free brochures, posters, and pencils grabbed as popular keepsakes. The downside of indoor truck shows is that local fire and safety regulations restrict drivers from starting the truck engines. In fact, diesel fuel tanks often are drained.

Outdoor truck shows are very popular during the summer months. The available space and natural lighting are preferred by amateur and professional truck photographers alike. As Stan Holtzman, the photographer for this book, explains: "colors seem to come alive in outdoor truck shows." Of course, there is nothing like standing near a big rig as the engine is fired. The roar of a Cummins, the smell of diesel, and the contrast of smoke against a bright sky add to the sensory experience of these events.

A 1953 LJ Mack can be seen here, fully restored for an Oregon truck show. Besides being just "another classic older truck," this is a working truck that hauled freight in and around the Albany area of Oregon.

A new International Eagle is seen here at the 1998 Mid-America Truck Show in Louisville, Kentucky. The Mid-America Truck Show is one of the largest in the world, and it is where truck makers bring out their best.

Truck shows can attract both new and older trucks. Here, a 1947 LT Mack is at an indoor truck show in Anaheim, California.

A future truck photographer is seen with his dad at a Washington truck show, checking out a neat 1955 Kenworth cab-over on display.

NEW, ANTIQUE, AND WORKING TRUCKS

There are three types of indoor and outdoor truck shows: those featuring new trucks, antique trucks, and working trucks. Original equipment manufacturers (OEMs) sponsor and pay for new truck shows. They target large fleets, other buyers, and national trade media. Getting the word out on new truck products is an important marketing aspect of new lines. Antique truck shows are held by national or regional chapters and feature the trucks of the past. Truck restoration has become a significant and costly endeavor. Working truck shows are often sponsored and operated by a charity. Some truck shows combine features of the new, antique, and working shows.

Working truck shows are controversial because it is not always clear how much of the money collected ends up in the hands of the charity. Further, it is difficult to define a working truck. For example, how many miles should a working truck have to be eligible for the show? If a truck is truly working on a daily basis, how can it be kept clean and polished enough to be competitive? Attendance at some of these shows can be fairly pricey: $10 admissions plus parking and refreshments can make it difficult for some who would like to see the big rigs. Our photographer Stan Holtzman has been told that some truckers shut down their rigs as much as one week in advance to compete. Questions also have been raised about judging, "payola," and compensation at some working truck shows. Still, truck shows are a fun way for truckers and the public to enjoy rigs together.

Many truck shows bring out only the local competition. Here we see two Internationals from Certified Grocers. The red unit features the older colors, and the white one is the company's current color scheme.

PERSONALIZED RIGS

Professional truckers like to personalize and show off their rigs. "All of the sudden, you realize your truck is just as beautiful as any other rig," says Linda Johnson. But it takes a lot of preparation to show a truck. There are financial issues related to being out of service for days at a time plus the costs of customizing. Then again, a show truck may be a great investment as a public relations tool. Show trucks are judged on appearance, design, finish, interior, and other factors, such as mileage. Once a truck has been customized, it is up to the driver to keep it looking sharp. Of course, a careful polishing job brings out the best in these mammoth machines. When you see a truck out on the road that sparkles and shines, look up and nod approval to the driver who takes pride in his or her work.

Truck shows can take place anywhere and in all sorts of weather. This W900L Kenworth was one of the many beautiful entries at the 1998 Mid-America Working Truck Show, which is held in Louisville around March of each year.

A contestant completes some final touches on one of Bill Frampton's Peterbilts at a truck show in Santa Nella, California. A lot of time, work, and expense can go into entering a big rig in a truck show, and for that reason every contestant should be given a meaningful prize by the various sponsors.

CHAPTER 14

ODDS AND ENDS
BEYOND TRACTORS

Now, as we enter the next 100 years, new technologies such as alternative power sources, satellite communications, and better diagnostic equipment, as well as the skills to use them, make this an exciting time for all those involved in the industry.

—Motor News (1999)

The American semi-truck, like all motor vehicles today, continues to be reinvented. New technologies and computer diagnostics have focused attention on century-old problems such as vehicle life, fuel efficiency, service and parts replacement, and design complexity. *Motor News* magazine predicts that "Styling will bring us even more radical new concepts in vehicle packaging than we are beginning to see now."

The truck, in its simplest view, is a tractor, or a cab, or an 18-wheeler. In reality, however, the semi-truck must be seen as the sum of its parts. We focus here on some of the interesting parts—trailers and tires—as well as some of the innovative uses of semis.

TRAILERS

Trailers, of course, provide storage for transported goods. Manufacturers such as Wabash, Fruehauf, and LBT emphasize low cost, maintenance, and durability in the sale of trailers. Lightweight aluminum and plastic construction have cut the weight of trailers in recent years by more than 1,000 pounds. This helps owners and drivers with fuel efficiency.

TIRES

Tires are one of the largest operating expenses for truckers, and they can have a dramatic impact on fuel efficiency. Goodyear, for example, has introduced its G302 fuel-efficient-drive (FED) tire. The company claims the tire may improve fuel efficiency by as much as 6 to 8 percent. The FED and other new tires employ shorter lug elements to reduce wear and new tread designs to improve traction. Fuel-efficient tires run cooler. According to Goodyear, "That's important because heat is a tire's worst enemy, especially when it comes to retreadability." In the end, the tire is what separates driver and truck from the road. It is what keeps the big rigs rolling.

This Kenworth W900L operates out of Conroe, Texas, and is dipped in enough chrome to get anyone's attention.

This 1940s Federal, owned by Chalker Bros. of San Bernardino, California, is more than just a truck: it is a tribute to the men and women whose lives it touched indirectly. This truck symbolizes a time when life and all of its gadgets were simpler.

UNUSUAL RIGS

For $87,000 Kingsley Coach of Houston will convert an old truck cab into a luxury recreational vehicle, using a 45-foot trailer bolted to the cab as a rigid unit. An aluminum box features "a full and half bath, shower, bedroom, kitchen, and a walk-through into the truck cab." The company will build the unusual RV from scratch for $325,000. "You get a five-year warranty on the living quarters and a half-million miles on the diesel cab's engine. And when you come ripping down the road behind that 600 horses of power, the others on the highway are bound to give you lots of room," said *Houston Chronicle* columnist Jim Barlow in 1998.

Dale Miller hauled cattle for Federal Meat Company of Vernon, California, in this open-top truck and trailer combination. From the 1930s until the early 1970s, this was the way livestock was transported out West. However, with the onset of the emergence of aluminum, livestock haulers could haul more critters in closed aluminum boxes and be more cost efficient.

Back in the 1940s and 1950s, a semi-trailer was usually no longer than 35 feet. This was due to strict length laws imposed by each state. Back then, a tractor-trailer or even a truck and trailer combination could not be more than 55 feet in overall length. Today, we see semi-trailers that are 55 feet long. This 1956 picture shows a 35-foot-long freight trailer on the old Anaheim-Telegraph Road, near the Santa Ana Freeway, in California.

Stainless-steel trailers, when properly maintained, present a badly needed positive image for the trucking industry. Helping improve this image is Great Dane, a maker of quality semi-trailers whose products can be seen in all parts of the United States.

Pictured here at a Shell Oil loading rack is a 1997 Freightliner truck and trailer. Weld-It Tank Manufacturing Company of Commerce, California, has been making quality truck bodies and trailers for the petroleum industry for over 50 years, with little notoriety or fanfare. This unit was speced out for delivering gasoline and diesel fuel through heavy Los Angeles traffic and into small gas stations.

Ralph Dickenson, owner of Kingsley Coach, said retired truckers like the idea of continuing to live on the road. He began building coaches out of buses, and has sold three to the father of country music star LeAnn Rimes. The Kingsley Coach is offered with a four-speed automatic transmission for those who don't want to jam gears. Because the rig is considered an RV, it can be driven on a standard license.

TV STUDIOS ON WHEELS

All major American television networks now use semi-trucks to transport mobile production facilities to major sporting events such as the NBA finals, the Rose Bowl, and the NCAA basketball championships. For example, a Kenworth pulled a Fox Sports truck in the late 1990s. The W900L hauled production equipment to the 1998 World Series and Super Bowl XXXIII. Owner Glenn Massung told

Overdrive magazine: "It might be glamorous compared to most trucking, but it gets pretty grueling . . . The schedule is hectic; it's just one game right after the other." A 51-foot trailer houses field cameras and cables in the rear; a computer graphics suite in the middle; and power units up front. Massung's Pittsburgh Mobile TV invested $500,000 in the 1996 Kenworth conventional, and his team of drivers logged more than 125,000 miles.

JUST FOR FUN

At Race City Motorsport Park in Calgary, turbocharged diesel engines powered big rigs around a half-mile, high-banked oval race track. These 12,000-pound Mack, Peterbilt, and Kenworth tractors with their 550-cubic-inch motors cranking out 600 horsepower became popular in the race circuit in the late 1990s. The first Oilpatch National big-rig race brought in more than 8,000 fans.

Rubber on the Road: Tires and American Trucking

Truck tires and wheels have come a long way since the first balloon tires appeared in the 1920s. Made with state-of-the-art materials, coupled with lightweight aluminum wheels, and running on better highways and interstates, today's truck tires are lasting longer, provided they receive regular maintenance.

In 1898, Frank Seiberling borrowed $3,500 from his brother-in-law, purchased a strawboard factory in East Akron, Ohio, added a $217.86 payroll, and started making tires for bicycles and carriages. The company also made fire hoses, sealing rings, and rubber poker chips. Today, Goodyear operates plants in 30 countries, has 105,000 employees, and has sales of more than $12 billion. Seiberling's statue of the Roman god Mercury inspired Goodyear to use its wingfoot logo as part of a 1901 Saturday Evening Post advertisement. Although the bicycle craze and the needs of the carriage industry spawned Goodyear, Seiberling had larger ideas. He offered young Henry Ford tires for his new race car. By 1903, the first tubeless automobile tire was patented. Goodyear was a pioneer in all-weather tread and pneumatic rubber tires. Goodyear expanded into Canada and Europe by 1912, the same year its first blimp appeared.

It was the 1917 Wingfoot Express, a Goodyear-sponsored trucking expedition from Akron to Boston, that helped show the nation that cross-country trucking was feasible. The 1920s brought off-road tire development and helped Goodyear become the world's largest tire and rubber company. Goodyear had a difficult time convincing truck manufacturers that they should buy pneumatic tires, so they built their own five- and six-ton trucks during the 1920s. One truck set a cross-country record by traveling from New York to Los Angeles in less than a week. Goodyear's fleet of Wingfoot Express trucks sent products from Akron to Boston, and pneumatic truck tires eventually became standard operating equipment.

By 1934, Goodyear had introduced earthmover tires and the first studded mud and snow tires. Goodyear's rubber rafts, floatation vests, and truck tires helped the nation go to and win World War II. Goodyear continued to play a leadership role in product development and marketing of tires on a global scale. Along the way, Goodyear acquired Kelly Springfield Tire Company and Dunlop. Goodyear maintained its independence during the 1980s and was the first Western tire company to open a store in Beijing, China, in 1993. $1 billion "global alliance" with Sumitomo Rubber created joint ventures in Japan, Europe, and North America. "Since our founding," says Goodyear CEO Samir Gibara, "we have always tried to reach further to bring new quality products to our customers." Goodyear's G302 truck tire features up to 32-inch tread depth and reduced heel and toe wear. The company goal is to improve the appearance and traction of truck tires, even as they wear. The newest tires run cooler and last longer.

Two years after Frank Seiberling started Goodyear, Harvey Firestone, a 31-year-old inventor, started production with 12 employees in Akron. On the other side of the globe, Shojiro Ishibashi moved from footwear to tires and became Japan's first manufacturer. Bridgestone of Japan would eventually merge with Firestone in 1988. Four years later, Firestone headquarters moved from Akron to Nashville. Today, the company boasts 38 plants, 1,500 retail stores, 45,000 employees, and sales of 50 million tires a year.

Truck tires and wheels have come a long way since the first truck tires touched down on the narrow streets of America. What cannot be overlooked are the advancements that were and are still being made in truck-tire repairing. While it may still be physically challenging to repair the tires on an 18-wheeler, the use of better machines, more hydraulic power, and less muscle power means less physical toil and injury in this specialized area that is often taken for granted.

"They're wonderful affairs, and they're fun. It's very unique," Peter Van Dyck of Airdrie told the *Calgary Herald* in 1998. His hot-pink Peterbilt was a crowd-pleaser. "I can do 360s with my truck, and smoke the tires like a Funny Car." Swervin' Mervin Pidherney set the Race City lap record of 21.68 seconds. His T800 Kenworth was powered by a computerized C12 Caterpillar engine. "I love NASCAR, so I'm really into racing, period, but when one of these is over, I can't wait for the next one."

BELLS AND WHISTLES

It might seem like a minor detail, but the driver's seat on a semi-truck is really important. In 1998, Freightliner introduced the Big Daddy seat. It offers an extra-wide cushion design, added support, and a wide and adjustable headrest. A pulsar massage, heating unit, and adjustable armrests are optional. Freightliner's Big Daddy is built on a "maintenance-free" pedestal. Its shock absorber minimizes the bumpy ride.

Today's modern semis feature luxury interiors, comfortable sleepers, and plenty of access to technology. Satellite television and cellular telephone systems keep drivers plugged in while on the road. And the rapidly advancing use of onboard computer systems suggests that the truck of the twenty-first century will be high tech.

ABOVE: *This 1986 Freightliner was originally just another truck and trailer in the large fleet of trucks owned by Swift Transportation of Phoenix, Arizona. However, with the aid and expertise of George Sack of Agua Dulce, California, this bobtail was converted into a portable pizzeria, making pizzas at sports events and wherever large crowds gather.*

This 1961 fully armor-plated Hendrickson is powered by a Cummins 250-horsepower engine. Hendrickson is famous for making the unusual in the trucking industry.

There are long hoods and then there are really *long hoods, as on this 1950s vintage Peterbilt, owned by Western Distributing of Denver, Colorado. By extending the hood of an already long hood convention, Western has achieved what they wanted: an attention-getter.*

This armor-plated unit is at a Las Vegas truck wash. It is a 1988 International with a 350-horsepower Cummins supplying the power. This rig runs between Los Angeles and Salt Lake City, carrying paper money, food stamps, coins, and other negotiable items. If you think this would be an easy heist, you better think again. The three guys on board have enough firepower to hold an entire SWAT team at bay.

In this 1967 picture, a White-Freightliner circa 1951 is seen as a "Tiltin' Hilton." With the sleeper located above the driver, it has more payload space, and this application worked for the livestock haulers of the 1950s. This rig may have been part of the Al Scannavino fleet of livestock trucks that operated out of Stockton, California, in the 1950s.

Wabash Fruehauf and Truck Trailers

The manufacture of semi-truck trailers has been central to the development of truck transportation in America. Today, Wabash Incorporated in Indiana is a leader in the construction of aluminum plate truck trailers. Wabash trailers are more durable and have more interior space than the cheaper aluminum sheet-and-post trailers. Wabash had 20 percent of the truck trailer market in 1997 when it purchased the once-leading Fruehauf Trailer, buried in debt with only 4 percent of the market, for $52 million. The enlarged Wabash now had more than $1 billion in revenue. Wabash Fruehauf's network of 31 retail outlets allowed the company to aggressively market its newest trailers that are as much as 1,000 pounds lighter than previous models because of composite plastic walls. The story of how Fruehauf went from leader to loser to leader is a tale of mismanagement that amazingly led to the reemergence of this famous brand name.

A Peterbilt wide-hood is seen here pulling a set of "Rocky Mountain doubles" for T. A. S. Trucking of Nampa, Idaho. This unusual configuration is seen in the Rocky Mountains of Idaho, Colorado, Nevada, Utah, and Wyoming.

During the late 1970s, Fruehauf, one of the giants in the semi-trailer business, found itself in a state of upheaval. In 1975 company chairman W. E. "Bill" Grace and president and chief executive officer Robert Rowan were convicted of conspiring to defraud the government of $12 million in taxes owed by Fruehauf. It was a major victory for the government, and marked the first time this kind of tax case had been brought against a publicly held firm. The two never served jail time. Instead, in 1979 shareholders reinstated Grace and Rowan by an overwhelming vote after their convictions on tax fraud.

It is hard to believe that in 1986 Fruehauf was the nation's largest maker of truck trailers, with sales of $2.5 billion a year. In 1989 Terex Corporation bought Fruehauf in a highly leveraged buyout. The lack of cash or credit left Fruehauf close to death. Trailer owners sometimes found it tough to get spare parts for repairs. The company borrowed $74 million at a time when interest rates were nearly 15 percent. Losses mounted year after year, and sales dropped to 10 percent of what they had been. By 1993 Fruehauf was barely holding on as the ninth-largest trailer maker. "Fruehauf really went to hell and back," said Herbert Lust III, a trucking-industry analyst at Furman Selz.

In 1993, Thomas Roller was named president and chief executive and given the job of halting the free fall. By 1994, Fruehauf returned as the fifth-largest trailer maker. Fruehauf had closed 38 plants and left open only manufacturing in Iowa and Tennessee. At the same time, it managed to develop a new trailer designed to cut owner costs by 40 percent. They named it the Phoenix, after the mythical bird that rises from the ashes. But Fruehauf's recovery was brief. Its financial problems ultimately led to a reorganization plan that left Fruehauf in the more capable hands of Wabash. It now appears that Fruehauf trailers will survive the rocky road.

The purchase of Fruehauf by Wabash helped the Indiana company remain a leading trailer manufacturer. The combined Wabash and Fruehauf brands were again profitable by the end of the 1990s. Today, the company appears to be the leading manufacturer of composite and aluminum plate trailers. Its wholly owned subsidiary, Fruehauf Trailer Services, is a leader in sales of new and used trailers and parts. About one of every five trailers on the road today is a Fruehauf, so the parts business is important.

The 1998 Fruehauf reorganization plan, called the "End of the Road Trust," helped end the Fruehauf financial nightmare. The plan paid creditors by using profits from a Mexico City plant. The 1997 sale of Fruehauf's manufacturing and sales business to Wabash brought the Fruehauf creditors $19 million in cash and another $17 million in Wabash stock. While Wabash agreed to hire many of the 1,300 Fruehauf employees, it did so without union contracts. Some 110,000 Fruehauf creditors filed a whopping $3.8 billion in claims.

Truck trailer manufacturers that survived the trucking downturn of the mid-1990s were rewarded with a booming economy at the end of the decade. While companies such as Wabash saw their stock prices fall, lack of debt was the key to survival as profits and stock prices eventually improved.

(Sources: "Fruehauf Corp. Top Executives are Reinstated," The Washington Post, June 8, 1979, p. F3; "The Wabash way," Forbes, April 6, 1998, p. 7, p. 78; John Taylor, "LBT Plant Labor Talks Canceled," Omaha World-Herald, July 6, 1999, p. 14; PR Newswire, May 6, 1998.)

In this 1970 picture we see an F Model Mack that was specially built to assist the BART System (Bay Area Rapid Transit) in San Francisco, California, should any mechanical breakdown or accident occur. This rig can either ride the rails or run on solid ground.

This one-of-a-kind 1964 Peterbilt cab-over was actually built in Portland, Oregon, by Pierce Auto Body Company. Because of its width, it required a three-piece windshield. It has twin-steering front axles and an Allison transmission to back up the V-12 engine. Needless to say, fuel mileage was not a top priority for this unit.

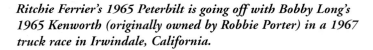

Ritchie Ferrier's 1965 Peterbilt is going off with Bobby Long's 1965 Kenworth (originally owned by Robbie Porter) in a 1967 truck race in Irwindale, California.

Curly Taylor of Manse Manufacturing in Pahrump, Nevada, makes pickup trucks look like their bigger brothers. These smaller-sized big rigs are a favorite at truck shows.

Dale Callen of San Marcos, California, created the comforts of home by making his Peterbilt a mobile home. This rig has all of the amenities that one would want, but in a truck. This rig has been seen at many truck shows.

The Destroyer is a 1969 White-Freightliner doing a little "auto recycling" at a Las Vegas truck show.

This long-wheelbased Peterbilt is "totally dedicated" to turning heads as it runs from Nebraska to California.

Bob Wilson of Montebello, California, owns "Old Ironsides," a long-hood Kenworth. Critics say that this truck's chrome and pinstriping is overkill but, as they say, "Beauty is in the eye of the beholder."

Leonard and Charlene Testerman of Maryland take Rollin' Thunder to as many truck shows as is practical. This wide-hood is a working rig, as well as being one nice piece of equipment.

John Pizzo of Bismarck, North Dakota, owns this purple people pleaser. This International features a Double Eagle sleeper with everything, including the kitchen sink.

This W900L Kenworth is part of the famous Showcase Fleet of good-looking rigs pulling for Allied Van Lines. Allied's Showcase fleet consists of only the best.

This trucker does not believe in advertising for the truck manufacturer, so no references to the truck maker appear. Think that is unusual? When was the last time you saw a United Parcel Service truck with a nameplate on it? Unlike the UPS trucks, this rig has just the right stuff on it to get the attention that it deserves.

This early-1980s Peterbilt shows what a neat-looking wrecker should look like. This "Pete" was based in Barstow, California, and sported a chrome Caterpillar engine under its hood.

CHAPTER 15

EPILOGUE

There is no such thing as a world truck . . .
There never has been and never will be.
—Freightliner CEO James Hebe (1998)

We have seen how trucks and trucking grew from the desire to ship products to new markets, and how the truck quickly surpassed the train as the preferred method of shipping. We have also seen how various truck manufacturers designed and redesigned the American semi-truck. In this final chapter, we look at the trends for future design.

CONTINUING SAFETY ISSUES

The continuing portrayal in our news and entertainment of truckers as outlaws willing to violate speed limits and government weight limits will no doubt fuel future efforts to legislate safety. Some people see each new crash involving a semi-truck as "evidence" that more regulation is needed. Others, however, interpret the statistics to mean that the nation's roads are safer than ever before. While safety issues remain on the agenda, a booming economy helped promote the idea that less regulation produces a more efficient marketplace.

FORCES AGAINST LONGER VEHICLES

Truck manufactures seeking to survive in the new global economy must be willing to address a number of design issues. At what point, particularly in the American West, is a truck and trailer rig too long? Triples, which allow for hauling more product on a single load, place extra stress on tractors and roads. Extra-long rigs raise safety issues as well. And operators must weigh fuel economy concerns in making decisions.

POWER, SPEED, AND MIGHT

American semi-trucks, if we can use the past to predict the future, will continue to increase in horsepower. Bigger is better in a competitive industry where time is money. At the same time, pollution and traffic congestion on the nation's interstate highway system and in our cities may become powerful forces that govern the rate of evolution.

A Volvo with an integral sleeper has a boatload of boats on board. This particular model is popular in Europe and was seen in Las Vegas. Does this mean that the European trucks are about to become an influential force in the American marketplace?

A CHP (California Highway Patrol) motor officer checks the log book of a household carrier. Every state has an agency that checks the amount of hours behind the wheel that drivers, both intra and interstate, have accrued.

Trucker Gary Rawson, driving for Parton Oil Company (no longer in business), proudly wears his Safe Driver buckle. Incentives for doing a good job should not go unnoticed. This buckle is just one way to tell a trucker that he is doing a good job.

The truck of tomorrow will continue to evolve, however, perhaps most impacted by the forces of information computer technology. The onboard computer systems on trucks of the future will no doubt shock truckers from the last century. Computers will improve communication between trucker and company, and they will also allow for monitoring of trucker behavior. This may place more responsibility in the hands of people outside the cab.

GLOBAL ECONOMIC FORCES

It is clear from the developments of the 1990s that America is experiencing a European invasion in the trucking and automotive industry. As export markets have become important to American truck manufacturers, so too has America come to embrace imported brands such as Mercedes Benz and Volvo. Global companies have a history of opening plants in America. So, in this century, it may become difficult to define what qualifies as an American semi-truck.

MERCEDES-BENZ

Karl Benz founded his company in 1883 with two others businessmen who wanted to build and sell industrial engines. When Gottlieb Daimler displayed his "steel-wheeled car" at the World Exhibition in Chicago in 1893, Benz premiered his "Velo." They were ahead of the Americans. By 1898, they were manufacturing four-cylinder 12-horsepower trucks in small numbers. Today, more than one hundred years later, Mercedes Benz remains a world leader. The Actros model is targeted at long-distance trucking. The Atego and the Econic series trucks round out the Mercedes line.

VOLVO

Sales of Volvo trucks increased in North America by 22 percent between 1998 and 1999. Volvo made large investments in engine plants in Brazil and Belgium, and the company standardized production lines with interchangeable parts. According to Volvo president Karl-Erling Trogen:

MORE THAN 90 PERCENT OF SALES VOLUME IS ACCOUNTED FOR BY TRUCKS WITH A GROSS VEHICLE WEIGHT OF MORE THAN 16 TONS. IN THIS CLASS, VOLVO TRUCKS' PRODUCT DEVELOPMENT IS BASED ON A SO-CALLED MODULAR CONCEPT, WHICH MEANS THAT THE SAME COMPONENTS ARE USED IN A NUMBER OF MODEL FAMILIES. THIS APPROACH RESULTS IN FEW COMPONENTS, A HIGH LEVEL OF FLEXIBILITY IN THE INDUSTRIAL SYSTEM, AND THE POTENTIAL FOR CUSTOMER ADAPTATION, AS WELL AS CREATING AN EXCELLENT BASE FOR TOP-CLASS QUALITY.

Volvo's truck production began in 1928, after the company was founded in Gothenburg, Sweden. Volvo, already in 120 world markets, has targeted new markets in Eastern Europe, China, and India. The 23,000 Volvo employees are taught the company's core values: quality, safety, and environmental concern.

EUROPEAN MODELS

Freightliner's use of diesel engines from parent DaimlerChrysler in medium and heavy trucks did not appear to signal a sea change;

From Roots to NAFTA and Beyond: The Road Ahead

Teamsters are seen here on strike at a P.I.E. terminal. P.I.E. has long been out of business, due, in part, to union demands.

"Virtually every necessity of our daily lives—food, clothing, housing—comes to us through some form of transportation," wrote historian Gerald Eskow in 1964. "The motor vehicle came into history in response to a need felt through the centuries, indeed millennia: to find an efficient and economical way to travel by road," author John Rae said. According to author A. M. Weimer, "The rise of the trucking industry is one of the great business evolutions of our time."

Who could have imagined trucking's humble beginnings leading to a major industry? In the seventeenth century gunners in Europe called the use of wheels under a sled a "trucke." In America, by the late eighteenth century, the word truck also meant a load of produce. The development of the internal combustion engine changed all that, according to historian William Childs: "The nature of trucking was basically individualistic—one driver, one truck."

"To refer to the driver as trucking's key man is not an overstatement," Gerald Eskow concluded. "Over the years the public image of the driver has been vastly distorted. Far from being the stereotyped muscle-bound manual laborer, today's driver must be a man of skill and maturity." James Thomas added that the trucker is an icon. "The trucker has a position unique in American history and mythology." Still, every myth has its origins, and this one comes from rugged individualists: "As independent businessmen," wrote scholars Daryl Wyckoff and David Maister, "among the most vigorously independent in America, the owner-operators are often highly resented by the Teamsters Union and many larger truck lines, and they are often a problem to government agencies." Wyckoff later concluded: "Truck drivers form one of the largest indirectly supervised workforces in the United States."

Changes came toward the end of the twentieth century for truckers, according to policy analysts Paul Teske, Samuel Best, and Michael Mintrom: "For most of this century, the federal and state governments heavily regulated freight transportation." As major truck manufacturers emerged, as the government sponsored mammoth road construction efforts such as the Interstate Highway Act, as truck engines and technology improved, as fuel efficiency became a central cost issue because of the fuel shortages of the 1970s, as truckers went cross-country, and as the economy went global, change was inevitable. Significantly, labor unions, such as the Teamsters, took on less importance. The North American Free Trade Agreement (NAFTA) was the first salvo in a battle for free markets and global competition. Sparked by the deregulation of the 1980s and 1990s, NAFTA gave the trucking industry new flexibility. But this came at a price because it also meant less government market protections. It remains to be seen how trucks will evolve to meet these new challenges, how trucking companies will adapt to new conditions, and how truck drivers will react to the role that computer technology will play in their lives. As Henry Ford observed long ago, "We have only started on our development of our country—we have not as yet, with all our talk of wonderful progress, done more than scratch the surface."

No matter what the future will be for the American semi-truck, it is safe to say that it will survive in some form as needed by the economy. Out there somewhere are youngsters whose dreams are made from the power of the vehicle, just as writer Lawrence Oulett remembers: "When I was a youngster, trucking captured my imagination . . . the hugeness of the vehicles, the lights that covered some of them like Christmas trees, the danger, the cafes and motels and truck stops, the driver-to-driver signaling . . . this was the stuff of high adventure."

A 1998 International can be seen along Interstate 15, just south of Salt Lake City. Trucking is more efficient when one tractor and one driver can move more goods using multiple trailers. Those concerned with highway safety say that these multiple units are too long and unsafe for the highways.

An older Diamond T is on the Clayton dynamometer at Motor Truck Distributors in the 1960s. The "dyno" can measure the exact horsepower being put to the ground.

Freightliner continued to offer diesels from other makers. But industry experts agreed that truck technology standards are needed. Daimler diesels, for example, required a new package of electronics before they could be made compatible with Freightliner's trucks. As truck engines and drivetrains take on more sophisticated computer controls, and as vehicles use personal wireless communications systems to stay linked to factories and warehouses, software has become a major issue. "I think we are just now beginning to understand what's possible and what the challenges are," said James Henderson, CEO of Cummins Engine Co. Some companies view proprietary technology as a competitive edge and are wary of being constrained by industry-wide standards. But fleets and truck owners want standards that simplify operations and cut costs. The European influence, however, may produce a more complex vehicle.

THE FUTURE OF THE BIG RIG

The future continues to look bright for the American semi-truck because it fits the American way of doing business. The truck, like the automobile, symbolizes freedom and flexibility. As the information technology sector exploits global e-commerce, truckers will continue to deliver the goods.

The truck of the future may be defined by lighter-weight construction materials, innovative onboard computer systems, and greater emphasis on driver comfort. Class 8 truck sales were down and then up again during the last decade of the twentieth century. The new world marketplace is the key to trucking's second century.

As truck designs become more aerodynamic for greater fuel efficiency, future big rigs might look like this. So all of you truckers running "large cars" better put them up on blocks, park them in some barn, and let them become valuable collector vehicles.

A 1990 Renault is seen at a truck show in Anaheim, California. Renault was the parent company of Mack Trucks. Will the European trucks become popular with American truckers? Only time will tell.

BIBLIOGRAPHY

Broehl, Wayne G., Jr. *Trucks . . . trouble . . . and triumph: The Norwalk Truck Line Company*. New York: Arno Press, 1976.

Cain, Wilma W. *Story of Transportation*. Grand Rapids, MI: Gateway Press, 1988.

Childs, William R. *Trucking and the Public Interest: The Emergence of Federal Regulation 1914–1940*. Knoxville: The University of Tennessee Press, 1985.

Chrysler Corporation: The Story of an American Company. Detroit: Chrysler Corporation, 1955.

Eskow, Gerald. *Your Future in the Trucking Industry*. New York: Richards Rosen Press, 1964.

Ford, Henry. *My Life and Work*. New York: Arno Press, 1973, 1922.

Glaskowsky, Nicholas A. *Effects of Deregulation on Motor Carriers*. Westport, CT: ENO Foundation for Transportation, 1986.

Holtzman, Stan. *Semi-Truck Color History*. Osceola, WI: MBI Publishing Company, 1997.

Holtzman, Stan. *American Semi Trucks*. Osceola, WI: MBI Publishing Company, 1995.

Johnson, Linda S. *Overdrive's Pride & Polish Manual*. Tuscaloosa, AL: Randall Publishing, 1996.

Leffingwell, Randy. *The American Farm Tractor*. Osceola, WI: MBI Publishing Company, 1991.

Managing Speed: Review of Current Practice for Setting and Enforcing Speed Limits. Transportation Research Board, National Research Council, Special Report 254. Washington, DC: National Academy of Sciences, 1998.

Marston, Hope Irvin. *Big Rigs*. New York: Cobblehill Books, 1998.

Ouellet, Lawrence J. *Pedal to the Metal: The Work Lives of Truckers*. Philadelphia: Temple University Press, 1994.

Pound, Arthur. *The Turning Wheel: The Story of General Motors Through Twenty-five Years, 1908–1933*. Garden City, NY: Doubleday, Doran & Company, 1934.

Rae, John B. *The American Automobile Industry*. Boston: Twayne Publishers, 1984.

Teske, Paul, Samuel Best, and Michael Mintrom. *Deregulating Freight Transportation: Delivering the Goods*. Washington, DC: The AEI Press, 1995.

Thomas, James H. *The Long Haul: Truckers, Truck Stops & Trucking*. Memphis, TN: Memphis State University Press, 1979.

Wagner, Rob Leicester. *Kings of the Road: A Pictoral History of Trucks*. New York: MetroBooks, 1997.

Wyckoff, Daryl D. *Truck Drivers in America*. Lexington, MA: Lexington Books, 1979.

Wyckoff, Daryl D. *Organizational Formality and Performance in the Motor-Carrier Industry*. Lexington, MA: Lexington Books, 1974.

Wyckoff, Daryl D., and David H. Maister. *The Motor-carrier Industry*, 1977.

Wyckoff, Daryl D., and David H. Maister. *The Owner-operator: Independent Trucker*. Lexington, MA: Lexington Books, 1975.

GLOSSARY

Alligator: A strip of retreaded tire seen alongside the highway.

Backhaul: A return trip with a loaded trailer or truck body.

B-trains: Canadian doubles (different from their U.S. counterparts).

Big rig: The largest trucks on the highway, a semi-truck is normally a 10-wheel tractor pulling an 8-wheel trailer.

Bobtail: A tractor driven without a trailer attached. Also, a straight truck, used in city pickup and delivery.

Boom wagon: A load of explosives.

Cab: The part of the tractor or truck where the driver sits.

Centipede: A trailer with many axles to support greater weight.

Common carrier: A company in the business of transporting goods for a wide range of companies.

Doubles: A tractor pulling two trailers.

Drom: A box, flatbed truck that can carry extra payload, located between the back of the cab and fifth wheel (dromedary).

Fifth wheel: The round plate and hinge on the tractor that locks the trailer in place.

Flatbed: Flat surface platform trailer or truck body.

Less than truckload (LTL): Typically a load less than 10,000 pounds and not requiring truckload rates, consigned to several customers.

Long nose: Conventional tractor with the engine in front of the cab and an extra-long hood.

Lowboy: A "gooseneck" trailer built low to the ground for hauling oversized cargo.

Owner operator: An individual who owns his or her truck.

Possum belly: A drop-frame trailer with floor level below the axles, popular with livestock and furniture haulers.

Private carrier: A company that owns its own trucks.

Pup: A short trailer.

Reefer: A refrigerated van trailer or truck body.

Semi-trailer: A trailer with one or more axles and typically eight wheels that rest on a tractor.

Sleeper: A built-in bed in the back of a tractor cab.

Snubnose: Cab-over-engine (COE) that tilts for access to the engine.

Tanker: A bottlelike trailer for hauling liquids.

Trailer: Semi-trailers usually have no front wheels (except for the trailer of a truck and trailer) and are pulled by the tractor.

Tractor: The truck or "power unit" that pulls the trailer. The tractor has 10 wheels and typically pulls an 8 wheel trailer, hence the term "18 wheeler."

Truck and trailer: The payload is carried on the truck's frame, and the truck also hauls a pull-trailer—very popular in the American West.

Triples: A tractor pulling a semi-trailer and two short pup trailers.

Truckload (TL): The amount of freight required to fill a trailer.

Van: An enclosed semi-trailer.

INDEX